Understanding James

Using Semitic Bible Study Methods with a new foundation

Michael H. Koplitz

Sandra J. Koplitz

Table of Contents

Introduction

When a person is baptized as an infant and grows up in the church, their religious DNA assimilates different paradigms. The church has a message to give about Jesus Christ and His importance. Very few people study the theology and doctrines of the church to determine for themselves the accuracy of the church. The Proto-Orthodox church, which survived the pressures of the Roman Empire, decided to oppose any expression of Christianity that did not fit its dogma in its infancy. In addition, the Proto-Orthodox church would permanently destroy any writings that the rival Christians had developed.

The Gnostic Christians of Northern Egypt viewed the life of Jesus of Nazareth in a completely different way than the Proto-Orthodox church did. They saw the message about the Kingdom of Heaven as the vital purpose of Jesus. His birth, death, and resurrection are not mentioned in the Gnostic Gospels. However, did the Proto-Orthodox church destroy the Gnostic Gospels when they crushed said movement? The answer is yes and no. Yes, they destroyed what they got their hands on. No, because in 1948, copies of the Gnostic religious books were discovered in Alexandria, Egypt. Once these documents were translated, the world learned what the Gnostic Christians believed. It is fascinatingly different than what the Proto-Orthodox said about these followers of Christ.

Why is this understanding critical? Much research points to a different situation in the early years than what the church espouses. A lot of this information is available to anyone today. However, the Seminaries and churches will not openly discuss these other writings about Jesus and His disciples. The scholars teaching in most Seminaries have learned their lessons from the church and closed-minded mentors who refuse to look at other possibilities. This is because the Western European world took Christianity and changed it from a Near Eastern religion to Western religion.

There is a theory that Paul converted Mithras House Churches into Jesus House Churches. This is clear from the connection between the Mithras' and Christianity's rituals. For example, baptism was the initiation ritual of Mithras. Communion did not originate with Jesus. This ritual was a part of Mithras, where the followers would share his flesh (bread) and drink his blood (wine). There are many more rituals that Christianity picked up from Mithras. A good reference is "Christianity's Need for Mithras," which the author wrote.

Did Paul create the churches in the letters he sent, which comprise the New Testament, and if so, they must have been Jewish groups who became Jewish Christians? They would have continued with their Hebraic rituals and saw Jesus of Nazareth as the Messiah that the prophets of old had promised. They would have adopted many of Jesus' teachings and tried to live by them. The letters in the New Testament are written in Greek. However, most Jews in the Roman Empire did not speak Greek; instead, they spoke Aramaic and Hebrew. These congregations would not have understood a Greek letter from Paul.

Therefore, the letters in the New Testament must have been written in Aramaic and then transliterated into Greek. The same can be said for the Gospels, all of them. The church, over the centuries, decided who wrote the Gospels and their intent. The only Gospel we can assign to a writer is Luke. The other three are up in the air about who wrote them. While in Seminary, the author was taught that the entire New Testament was originally written in Koine Greek. However, that raised the question, "Did Jesus speak Greek?" The Seminary instructors says, "no, Jesus did not speak Greek." Then the New Testament, especially the Gospels, must have been written in Aramaic. After all, Jesus spoke Aramaic and Hebrew.

We know this because He was a poor *tekton* (a stonemason or carpenter) from an impoverished city named Nazareth. Being born to a Jewish family in Galilee, he would have learned the traditions of His people and trade. He would have learned to speak Aramaic, the language of the area. He would have learned Hebrew because that was the language of the synagogue and the Temple in Jerusalem. In other words, Hebrew was the language of God, and Jewish males learned the language.

Suppose you are ready to toss this manuscript into the nearest trash can or delete it off your electronic device at this point in the introduction. In that case, the writer has your attention. This is the reaction when the writer has spoken with persons who had been indoctrinated into the church's position since birth. The author did not come into the church environment until he was 35. Therefore, the church's paradigms, dogma, and doctrine were not a part of his DNA. Instead, he questioned a lot. He found many inconsistencies between the Bible and the doctrines of the church. Seminary was an experience to learn what the church had evolved into two-thousand years after the death of Jesus.

There are more parts to the premise that the New Testament was originally written in Aramaic and will be explored. For the reader to grasp the subsequent phases of the proof, an open mind is critical.

Culture and Language

Let us continue in the journey of examining the New Testament to determine its original language. Nothing in stone tells us that Aramaic is the Original Language of the New Testament. However, nothing says that Koine Greek was the original language of the New Testament either. Therefore, we have two theories about the original language of the New Testament. The author admits that the Seminary he attended drove home the belief that the Old Testament was written in Hebrew, except for a few spots. The New Testament was initially written in Koine Greek.

The writers' research has been searching for the original meaning of Scripture for many years. The methodology for this work is called "Ancient Bible Study Methods." The method was developed by Dr. Anne Davis of the Bible Learning University in Albuquerque, New Mexico. The author studied this method with Dr. Davis as his mentor. It became clear that the search for the original meaning of the Scriptures requires that the culture and language be examined. So, the author's methodology is Dr. Davis' work, plus his Ph.D. studies combining the method, culture, and language.

The language examination is easy for the Old Testament because it was written in Hebrew, and about one-half of Daniel is in Aramaic. It does not take long to realize that idioms and figures of speech in the Hebrew of the Old Testament revealed a lot about the people and situation of the day when the scrolls were written. The Targums were a valuable resource because they are the Aramaic translations the rabbis did for the people living outside of Judea. The rabbis added commentary to the Targums because they knew that some of the idioms and speech used in the Near East would not translate well into the different areas where the Jews lived.

The culture of the Near East has been essentially the same in many aspects since the days of Jesus. Many practices of Jesus' day are still in use today. The culture of the Jews of the Near East is built into the language. Often an Aramaic or Hebrew word has a deep meaning that is only fully understood by natives living in that culture. The Old Testament is filled with cultural items that do not need to be spelled out because the people knew their culture in the author's time.

Suppose the New Testament in Koine Greek is a transliteration of the Aramaic. The culture, figures of speech, and idioms will be easily identified when examining the Peshitta (the Aramaic version of the New Testament). Indeed many of the so-called difficult words of Jesus are not tricky when examined in the light of the culture of Jesus' day. An example is "faith to move a mountain," Jesus says these words to His disciples. The church determined that this meant complete faith in Jesus. From the western European Greek point of view, that makes sense. What else could it possibly mean?

"Faith to move a mountain" is an Aramaic idiomatic expression. What Jesus says to His followers when he says this is that his disciples needed to be faithful so that they could change the "government's view through their words." The governing body for Judaism resided on the top of a mountain. Jerusalem, with its Temple, was built on the top of Mount Zion, a very tall mountain. This idiom survived because the Aramaic Gospels were transliterated into Koine Greek. Numerous other examples support this position.

Suppose the culture and language idioms of Jesus' day can be found in the Koine Greek because it was transliterated. In that case, it supports the theory of the Aramaic versions being the original language of the Gospels and possibly even more.

The Aramaic Version of the New Testament

The Peshitta is the accepted Aramaic translation of the New Testament for many churches of the East. Peshitta means "simple, true, direct, and original." It is a collection of scrolls that were compiled in 150 CE. There were some revisions to the Peshitta in the fifth and sixth centuries. The Greek version of the New Testament is a transliteration of the Peshitta.[1]

For centuries, the Catholic church has used the Latin version of the Bible, the Vulgate, and still uses it. The Vulgate was developed around 350 CE by Jerome by order of the Pope at that time. Erasmus (1466 – 1536) was the person who put together the Greek New Testament for the Catholic church.

"The New Testament, brought to light in the original Greek tongue, was compiled and made available for humanity to study and learn. Although working under and deeply associated with the Roman Catholic Church, the learned scholar declared his disagreement with those who wanted to keep the Scriptures from the common people. He said, "If only the farmer would sing something from them at his plow, the weaver moves his shuttle to their tune, the traveler lighten the boredom of his journey with Scriptural stories!" Little did he know that the work he was about to produce would change the world forever. This Greek New Testament, in printed form, would become the standard of the New Testament, launching the translations of Martin Luther and William Tyndale into the world. Thus, fulfilling his dream that all men would read the

---

[1] Rocco A. Errico and George M. Lamsa, *Aramaic Light on Galatians through Hebrews: A Commentary Based on Aramaic, the Language of Jesus, and Ancient near Eastern Customs* (Smyma, GA: Noohra Foundation, 2005).

Bible for themselves in their common language. His new "study Bible" had two main parts, the Greek text, and a revised Latin edition, which was more elegant and accurate than the traditional translation of Jerome's Latin Vulgate. Erasmus prefaced this monumental work of scholarship with an exhortation to Bible study. He proclaimed that the New Testament contains the "philosophy of Christ," simple and accessible teaching with the power to transform lives."[2]

The church recognized Erasmus' Greek New Testament in 1515 CE. The church in the Near East has been using the Peshitta as the original language of the New Testament since 150 CE. If the Greek New Testament was important to the church as an original language, then why did it adopt the Vulgate in 350 CE? The church should have adopted the Greek New Testament at the beginning.

The Peshitta, translated into English, is used to examine Paul's letters. The rest of the methodology that the author developed for Ancient Bible Study Methods is the framework of this research.

---

[2] "Erasmus Greek New Testament," Insight of the King, accessed February 18, 2022, https://www.insightoftheking.com/erasmus-greek-new-testament.html.

The Messianic Tradition Change

One problem for Peter and the Disciples was that they claimed Yeshua to be the Messiah that the prophets of the Hebrew Scriptures spoke. However, Yeshua did not do what these traditions said. The main tradition was that the Messiah would destroy oppressive Romans and reinstate the Kingdom of Israel. Yeshua would then be declared the king and sit on David's throne in Jerusalem. That did not occur.

None of the messianic traditions of the day worked. So, what was the new movement going to do? They turned to the prophets and discovered Isaiah 50-53. These chapters are referred to as the Suffering Servant chapters. The Yeshua movement decided that the Suffering Servant was Yeshua. The portrayal of Yeshua's life does fit the Suffering Servant chapters. However, rabbinical interpretation then and now sees the Suffering Servant as the nation of Israel. Indeed, these chapters do describe the history of Israel. Nations have wanted to destroy the Jewish people since the time of Abraham.

The diaspora from the Babylonia Exile and the Assyrian invasions looked to squelch the Jewish people. The LORD promised that a remnant of the people would always survive. That is true throughout the 4,000-year history of the Jewish people. Many nations tried to destroy them, and the LORD intervened to ensure that a remnant of the people survived.

Paul must have been convinced in his encounter with Yeshua on the Damascus road that Yeshua was the Suffering Servant. It is clear from Paul's writings that he did believe this. For Paul, the Messiah was the Spiritual Messiah that the Kabbalah spoke. The

Kabbalah says that there will be two Messiahs. This theology is based on Zachariah 9:9. The first Messiah is Messiah ben Joseph. This Messiah was to restore the Kingdom of Heaven, a spiritual Kingdom. The second Messiah will be Messiah ben David. This Messiah was to restore the Kingdom of Israel. The Midrash from the Kabbalah did not state that the Messiah was two different souls.

The Kabbalah

There is a large amount of material in print about the Kabbalah. The Kabbalah referred to is Moses's Secret Work from Mount Sinai. Legends say Moses received three items on Mount Sinai when he met the LORD. The first is the written law. The written law is called the Torah. The second is the oral law. The oral law was put into a written form around 200 CE called the Mishnah. The third is the secret law called the Kabbalah. The secrets of the Kabbalah are based on the Torah and were written down around 200 CE. The main books of the Kabbalah are the Zohar and the Book of Creation.

Many of Yeshua's statements have Kabbalah undertones. Yeshua would have known the Kabbalah. Paul would have known the basics, at least, of the Kabbalah because of his religious education and training.

There are Kabbalistic ideas in the Gospels and Paul's letters. Kabbalistic verses will be highlighted in the chapters of the letters.

Methodology

The methodology employed is to use "Ancient Bible Study Methods" integrated with Jesus's day's customs and culture to examine the Hebrew and Christian Scriptures, thus gathering a more in-depth understanding by learning the Scriptures in the way the people of Jesus's day did.

I have titled the methodology of analyzing a passage of Scripture in a Hebraic manner the "Process of Discovery." The author developed this methodology, which combines various linguistic and cultural understanding areas. There are several sections to the process, and not all the parts apply to every passage of Scripture. The overall result of developing this process is to give the reader a framework for studying the Word in more depth.

The "Process of Discovery" starts with a Scripture passage. An examination of the linguistic structure of the passage is next. The linguistic structure includes parallelism, chiastic structures, and repetition. Formatting the passage in its linguistic form allows the reader to visualize what the first-century CE listener was hearing. Their corresponding sections label the chiasms, for example, A, B, C, B', A.' Not all passages of the Scriptures have a poetic form.

The next step is to "question the narrative." The narrative process of questioning the narrative assumes the reader knows nothing about the passage. Therefore, the questions go from simple to complex. The next task is to identify any linguistic patterns. Linguistic patterns include, but are not limited to, irony, simile, metaphor, symbolism, idioms, hyperbole, figurative language, personification, and allegory.

A review of any translation inconsistencies discovered between the English NAU version and Hebrew or Greek versions is done. Sometimes, a Hebrew or Greek word is translated in more than one way. Inconsistencies also can be created by the translation committee, which may have decided to use traditional language instead of the actual translation. The decision of the translation committee is in the Preface or Introduction to the Bible. Perhaps some of the inconsistencies were intentionally added to convey some deeper meaning. An examination of every discrepancy is done.

The passage is analyzed for any echoes of the Hebrew Scriptures in the Christian Scriptures. An echo occurs using a passage from the Hebrew Scriptures in the Christian Scriptures.[3] Also, echoes are found when Torah (Genesis through Deuteronomy) passages are used in other Hebrew Bible books. Cross-references in the Scripture are references from one verse to another verse, which can help the reader understand the verse.

The names of persons mentioned in the passage are listed. Many Hebrew names have meaning and may be associated with places or actions. Jewish parents used to name their children based on what they felt God had in store for their children. An example is Abraham, whose original name was Abram and was changed to mean eternal father (God changed Abram's name to Abraham, indicating a function he was to perform). When the Hebrew Bible gives names, many occurrences mean something unique. The same importance can occur for the names of places. The time it takes to travel between locations can supply insight into the event.

---

[3] Mitzvot are the 613 commandments found in the Torah that please God. There are positive and negative commandments. The list was first development by Maimonides. The full list can be found at: ttp://www.jewfaq.org/613.htm.

Keyphrases are identified in verses when they are essential to understanding that passage. There are no rules for selecting the keywords. Searching for other occurrences of the keywords in Scripture in concordance is necessary to understand the Word's usage; this must be done in either Hebrew or Greek, not in English. A classic Hebraic approach is to find the usage of a word in the Scripture by finding other verses that contain the Word. The usage of a word in its original language is discovered by searching the Scripture in the language of the Word. Verses that contain the Word are identified, and a pattern for the usage of the Word is discovered. Each verse is examined to see what the usage of the Word is, which may reveal a model for the Word's usage. The first usage of the Word in the Scripture, primarily if used in the Torah, is essential for Hebrew words. The Christian Scriptures are used for Greek words to determine the Word usage in the Scripture. Sometimes, finding the equivalent Greek Word in the Septuagint can be beneficial as analyzing its Hebrew usage.

The Rules of Hillel are used when applicable. Hillel was a Torah scholar who lived shortly before Jesus' day. Hillel developed several rules for Torah students to interpret the Scriptures, which refer to halachic Midrash. In several cases, these rules are helpful in the analysis of the Scripture.

The cultural implications from the writing period are done after the linguistic analysis is completed. The culture is crucial because it is not explicitly referenced in the biblical narratives, as indicated earlier.

From the linguistic analysis and the cultural understanding, it is possible to obtain a deeper meaning of the Scripture beyond the plain text's literal meaning. That is what the listeners of Jesus's time were doing. They put linguistics and culture together without even having to contemplate it.

The analysis will lead to findings explaining the passage's meaning in Jesus's day. Most of the time, the Hebraic analysis leads to the desire for more in-depth analysis to fully understand what Jesus was talking about or what was happening to Him. Whatever the result, a new, more in-depth understanding of the Scripture is obtained.

The components of the Process of Discovery are:

Language

Process of Discovery

Linguistics Section

Linguistic Structure

Discussion

Questioning the Passage

Verse Comparison of citations or proof text

Translation Inconsistencies

Biblical Personalities

Biblical Locations

Phrase Study

Only the applicable sections are included in this document.

Introduction to the Epistle

The Book of James is a General Epistle (Apostolic Letter) in the New Testament of the Bible. It was likely the first New Testament book to be written, approximately around 48-49 A.D[1,2]. The author of this book is James, also known as James the Just, who is believed to be the half-brother of Jesus Christ[1].

The book is addressed to Jewish believers and encourages them to endure and live bold Christian lives. It is a practical guide on Christian living and reflects a genuine faith that transforms lives. In many ways, it is similar to the Old Testament book of Proverbs[1].

Here are some key themes and teachings from the book:

- Testing of Faith and Perseverance (James 1): James teaches believers to test their faith and encourages them to put their faith into action, and to be servants of Jesus Christ.
- Faith and Works (James 2-3): James describes the relationship between faith and works. He teaches that a person of faith without works demonstrates useless faith. He also teaches that everyone is a sinner and that if one of the 10 Commandments are broken, then that person is guilty of breaking every one of them.
- Wisdom and Instruction (James 4-5): James gives wise instruction to believers. He emphasizes the importance of submitting to God, resisting the devil, and the power of prayer. He uses the word "Prayer" 7 times, signifying its importance[1].

In essence, the Book of James is about practical Christian living that reflects a genuine faith that transforms lives. It encourages believers to be doers of the word, not just hearers, and promises blessings for their actions.[4]

---

[4] 1. James Summary, accessed April 29, 2024, https://biblehub.com/summary/james/1.htm.

Chapter One

Language

Peshitta	New American Standard 1995
James 1:1 James, a servant of God, and of our Lord Jesus the Messiah; to the twelve tribes dispersed among the Gentiles; greeting [peace]. **2** Let it be all joy to you, my brethren, when ye enter into many and various trials. **3** For ye know, that the trial of [your] faith, maketh you possess patience. **4** And let patience have its perfect work, so that ye may be complete and perfect, and may lack nothing. **5** And if any of you lacketh wisdom, let him ask [it] of God, who giveth to all freely, and reproacheth not; and it will be given him. **6** But let him ask in faith, not hesitating: he who hesitateth is like the waves of the sea, which the wind agitateth. **7** And let not that man expect to receive any thing of the Lord, **8** who is hesitating in his mind, and unstable in all his ways. **9** And let the depressed brother rejoice, in his elevation; **10** and the rich, in his depression; because, like the flower of an herb, so he passeth away. **11** For the sun riseth in its heat, and drieth up the herb; and its flower falleth, and the beauty of its appearance perisheth: so also the rich man withereth in his ways. **12** Blessed is the man who endureth temptations; so that when he is proved he may receive a crown of life, which God hath promised to them that love him. **13** Let no one when he is tempted, say, I am tempted of God: for God is not tempted with evils, nor doth he tempt any man. **14**	**James 1:1** [1a]James, a [b]bond-servant of God and [c]of the Lord Jesus Christ, To [d]the twelve tribes who are [2e]dispersed abroad: [f]Greetings. **James 1:2** [a]Consider it all joy, my brethren, when you encounter [b]various [1]trials, **3** knowing that [a]the testing of your [b]faith produces [1c]endurance. **4** And let [1a]endurance have *its* perfect [2]result, so that you may be [3b]perfect and complete, lacking in nothing. **James 1:5** But if any of you [a]lacks wisdom, let him ask of God, who gives to all generously and [1]without reproach, and [b]it will be given to him. **6** But he must [a]ask in faith [b]without any doubting, for the one who doubts is like the surf of the sea, [c]driven and tossed by the wind. **7** For that man ought not to expect that he will receive anything from the Lord, **8** *being* a [1a]double-minded man, [b]unstable in all his ways. **James 1:9** [a]But the [1]brother of humble circumstances is to glory in his high position; **10** and the rich man *is to glory* in his humiliation, because [a]like [1]flowering grass he will pass away. **11** For the sun rises with [1a]a scorching wind and [b]withers the grass; and its flower falls off and the

But every man is tempted by his own lust; and he lusteth, and is drawn away. **15** And this [his] lust conceiveth, and bringeth forth sin; and sin, when mature, bringeth forth death. **16** Do not err, my beloved brethren. **17** Every good and perfect gift cometh down from above, from the Father of lights, with whom is no mutation, not even the shadow of change. **18** He saw fit, and begat us by the word of truth; that we might be the first-fruits of his creatures. **19** And be ye, my beloved brethren, every one of you, swift to hear, and slow to speak; and slow to wrath: **20** for the wrath of man worketh not the righteousness of God. **21** Wherefore, remove far from you all impurity, and the abundance of wickedness; and, with meekness, receive the word that is implanted in our nature, which is able to vivify these your souls. **22** But be ye doers of the word, and not hearers only; and do not deceive yourselves. **23** For if any man shall be a hearer of the word, and not a doer of it, he will be like one who seeth his face in a mirror: **24** for he seeth himself, and passeth on, and forgetteth what a man he was. **25** But every one that looketh upon the perfect law of liberty and abideth in it, is not a hearer of something to be forgotten, but a doer of the things; and he will be blessed in his work. **26** And if any one thinketh that he worshippeth God, and doth not restrain his tongue, but his heart deceiveth him; his worship is vain. **27** For the worship that is pure and holy before God the Father, is this: to visit the fatherless and the widows in their affliction, and that one keep himself unspotted from the world.

beauty of its appearance is destroyed; so too the rich man in the midst of his pursuits will fade away.

James 1:12 [a]Blessed is a man who perseveres under trial; for once he has [1]been approved, he will receive [b]the crown of life which *the Lord* [c]has promises to those who [d]love Him. **13** Let no one say when he is tempted, ""I am being tempted [1]by God"; for God cannot be tempted [2]by evil, and He Himself does not tempt anyone. **14** But each one is tempted when he is carried away and enticed by his own lust. **15** Then [a]when lust has conceived, it gives birth to sin; and when [b]sin [1]is accomplished, it brings forth death. **16** [a]Do not be [1]deceived, [b]my beloved brethren. **17** Every good thing given and every perfect gift is [a]from above, coming down from [b]the Father of lights, [c]with whom there is no variation or [1]shifting shadow. **18** In the exercise of [a]His will He [b]brought us forth by [c]the word of truth, so that we would be [1]a kind of [d]first fruits [2]among His creatures.

James 1:19 [1]*This* [a]you know, [b]my beloved brethren. But everyone must be quick to hear, [c]slow to speak *and* [d]slow to anger; **20** for [a]the anger of man does not achieve the righteousness of God. **21** Therefore, [a]putting aside all filthiness and *all* [1]that remains of wickedness, in [2]humility receive [b]the word implanted, which is able to save your souls. **22** [a]But prove yourselves doers of the word, and not merely hearers who delude themselves. **23** For if anyone is a hearer of the word and not a doer, he is like a man who looks at his [1]natural face [a]in a mirror; **24** for *once* he has looked at

| | himself and gone away, [1]he has immediately forgotten what kind of person he was. **25** But one who looks intently at the perfect law, [a]the *law* of liberty, and abides by it, not having become a forgetful hearer but [1]an effectual doer, this man will be [b]blessed in [2]what he does.

James 1:26 If anyone thinks himself to be religious, and yet does not [1][a]bridle his tongue but deceives his *own* heart, this man's religion is worthless. **27** Pure and undefiled religion [a]in the sight of *our* God and Father is this: to [b]visit [c]orphans and widows in their distress, *and* to keep oneself unstained [1]by [d]the world. |
| --- | --- |

James 1:1
[1]Or *Jacob*
[2]Lit *in the Dispersion*
[a]Acts 12:17
[b]Titus 1:1
[c]Rom 1:1
[d]Luke 22:30
[e]John 7:35
[f]Acts 15:23

James 1:2
[1]Or *temptations*
[a]Matt 5:12; James 1:12; 5:11
[b]1 Pet 1:6

James 1:3
[1]Or *steadfastness*
[a]1 Pet 1:7
[b]Heb 6:12
[c]Luke 21:19

James 1:4
[1]V 3, note 1
[2]Lit *work*
[3]Or *mature*
[a]Luke 21:19
[b]Matt 5:48; Col 4:12

James 1:5
[1]Lit *does not reproach*
[a]1 Kin 3:9ff; James 3:17
[b]Matt 7:7

James 1:6
[a]Matt 21:21
[b]Mark 11:23; Acts 10:20
[c]Matt 14:28-31; Eph 4:14

James 1:8
[1]Or *doubting, hesitating*
[a]James 4:8
[b]2 Pet 2:14

James 1:9
[1]I.e. church member
[a]Luke 14:11

James 1:10
[1]Lit *the flower of the grass*
[a]1 Cor 7:31; 1 Pet 1:24

James 1:11
[1]Lit *the*
[a]Matt 20:12
[b]Ps 102:4, 11; Is 40:7f

James 1:12
[1]Or *passed the test*
[a]Luke 6:22; James 5:11; 1 Pet 3:14; 4:14
[b]1 Cor 9:25
[c]Ex 20:6; James 2:5
[d]1 Cor 2:9; 8:3

James 1:13
[1]Lit *from*
[2]Lit *of evil things*
[a]Gen 22:1

James 1:15
[1]Lit *is brought to completion*
[a]Job 15:35; Ps 7:14; Is 59:4
[b]Rom 5:12; 6:23

James 1:16
[1]Or *misled*
[a]1 Cor 6:9
[b]Acts 1:15; James 1:2, 19; 2:1, 5, 14; 3:1, 10; 4:11; 5:12, 19

James 1:17
[1]Lit *shadow of turning*
[a]John 3:3; James 3:15, 17
[b]Ps 136:7; 1 John 1:5
[c]Mal 3:6

James 1:18
[1]Or *a certain first fruits*
[2]Lit *of*
[a]John 1:13
[b]James 1:15; 1 Pet 1:3, 23
[c]2 Cor 6:7; Eph 1:13; 2 Tim 2:15
[d]Jer 2:3; Rev 14:4

James 1:19
[1]Or *Know* this
[a]1 John 2:21
[b]Acts 1:15; James 1:2, 16; 2:1, 5, 14; 3:1, 10; 4:11; 5:12, 19
[c]Prov 10:19; 17:27
[d]Prov 16:32; Eccl 7:9

James 1:20
[a]Matt 5:22; Eph 4:26

James 1:21
[1]Lit *abundance of malice*
[2]Or *gentleness*
[a]Eph 4:22; 1 Pet 2:1
[b]Eph 1:13; 1 Pet 1:22f

James 1:22
[a]Matt 7:24-27; Luke 6:46-49; Rom 2:13; James 1:22-25; 2:14-20

James 1:23
[1]Lit *the face of his birth;* or *nature*
[a]1 Cor 13:12

James 1:24
[1]Lit *and he*

James 1:25

[1]Lit *a doer of a work*
[2]Lit *his doing*
[a]John 8:32; Rom 8:2; Gal 2:4; 6:2; James 2:12; 1 Pet 2:16
[b]John 13:17

James 1:26
[1]Or *control*
[a]Ps 39:1; 141:3; James 3:2-12

James 1:27
[1]Lit *from*
[a]Rom 2:13; Gal 3:11
[b]Matt 25:36
[c]Deut 14:29; Job 31:16, 17, 21; Ps 146:9; Is 1:17, 23
[d]Matt 12:32; Eph 2:2; Titus 2:12; James 4:4; 2 Pet 1:4; 2:20; 1 John 2:15-17

Koine Greek

James 1:1   Ἰάκωβος, θεοῦ καὶ κυρίου Ἰησοῦ χριστοῦ δοῦλος, ταῖς δώδεκα φυλαῖς ταῖς ἐν τῇ διασπορᾷ, χαίρειν.

James 1:2   Πᾶσαν χαρὰν ἡγήσασθε, ἀδελφοί μου, ὅταν πειρασμοῖς περιπέσητε ποικίλοις, **3** γινώσκοντες ὅτι τὸ δοκίμιον ὑμῶν τῆς πίστεως κατεργάζεται ὑπομονήν· **4** ἡ δὲ ὑπομονὴ ἔργον τέλειον ἐχέτω, ἵνα ἦτε τέλειοι καὶ ὁλόκληροι, ἐν μηδενὶ λειπομενοι.**James 1:5**   Εἰ δέ τις ὑμῶν λείπεται σοφίας, αἰτείτω παρὰ τοῦ διδόντος θεοῦ πᾶσιν ἁπλῶς, καὶ οὐκ ὀνειδίζοντος, καὶ δοθήσεται αὐτῷ. **6** Αἰτείτω δὲ ἐν πίστει, μηδὲν διακρινόμενος· ὁ γὰρ διακρινόμενος ἔοικεν κλύδωνι θαλάσσης ἀνεμιζομένῳ καὶ ῥιπιζομένῳ. **7** Μὴ γὰρ οἰέσθω ὁ ἄνθρωπος ἐκεῖνος ὅτι λήψεταί τι παρὰ τοῦ κυρίου. **8** Ἀνὴρ δίψυχος, ἀκατάστατος ἐν πάσαις ταῖς ὁδοῖς αὐτοῦ.

James 1:9   Καυχάσθω δὲ ὁ ἀδελφὸς ὁ ταπεινὸς ἐν τῷ ὕψει αὐτοῦ· **10** ὁ δὲ πλούσιος ἐν τῇ ταπεινώσει αὐτοῦ· ὅτι ὡς ἄνθος χόρτου παρελεύσεται. **11** Ἀνέτειλεν γὰρ ὁ ἥλιος σὺν τῷ καύσωνι, καὶ ἐξήρανεν τὸν χόρτον, καὶ τὸ ἄνθος αὐτοῦ ἐξέπεσεν, καὶ ἡ εὐπρέπεια τοῦ προσώπου αὐτοῦ ἀπώλετο· οὕτως καὶ ὁ πλούσιος ἐν ταῖς πορείαις αὐτοῦ μαρανθήσεται.

James 1:12   Μακάριος ἀνὴρ ὃς ὑπομένει πειρασμόν· ὅτι δόκιμος γενόμενος λήψεται τὸν στέφανον τῆς ζωῆς, ὃν ἐπηγγείλατο ὁ κύριος τοῖς ἀγαπῶσιν αὐτόν. **13** Μηδεὶς πειραζόμενος λεγέτω ὅτι Ἀπὸ θεοῦ πειράζομαι· ὁ γὰρ θεὸς ἀπείραστός ἐστιν κακῶν, πειράζει δὲ αὐτὸς οὐδένα· **14** ἕκαστος δὲ πειράζεται, ὑπὸ τῆς ἰδίας ἐπιθυμίας ἐξελκόμενος καὶ δελεαζόμενος. **15** Εἶτα ἡ ἐπιθυμία συλλαβοῦσα τίκτει ἁμαρτίαν· ἡ δὲ ἁμαρτία ἀποτελεσθεῖσα ἀποκύει θάνατον. **16** Μὴ πλανᾶσθε, ἀδελφοί μου ἀγαπητοί. **17** Πᾶσα δόσις ἀγαθὴ καὶ πᾶν δώρημα τέλειον ἄνωθέν ἐστιν, καταβαῖνον ἀπὸ τοῦ πατρὸς τῶν φώτων, παρ' ᾧ οὐκ ἔνι παραλλαγή, ἢ τροπῆς ἀποσκίασμα. **18** Βουληθεὶς ἀπεκύησεν ἡμᾶς λόγῳ ἀληθείας, εἰς τὸ εἶναι ἡμᾶς ἀπαρχήν τινα τῶν αὐτοῦ κτισμάτων.

James 1:19   Ὥστε, ἀδελφοί μου ἀγαπητοί, ἔστω πᾶς ἄνθρωπος ταχὺς εἰς τὸ ἀκοῦσαι, βραδὺς εἰς τὸ λαλῆσαι, βραδὺς εἰς ὀργήν· **20** ὀργὴ γὰρ ἀνδρὸς δικαιοσύνην θεοῦ οὐ κατεργάζεται. **21** Διὸ ἀποθέμενοι πᾶσαν ῥυπαρίαν καὶ περισσείαν κακίας, ἐν πραΰτητι δέξασθε τὸν ἔμφυτον λόγον, τὸν δυνάμενον σῶσαι τὰς ψυχὰς ὑμῶν. **22** Γίνεσθε δὲ ποιηταὶ λόγου, καὶ μὴ μόνον ἀκροαταί, παραλογιζόμενοι ἑαυτούς. **23** Ὅτι εἴ τις ἀκροατὴς λόγου ἐστὶν καὶ οὐ ποιητής, οὗτος ἔοικεν ἀνδρὶ κατανοοῦντι τὸ πρόσωπον τῆς γενέσεως αὐτοῦ ἐν ἐσόπτρῳ· **24** κατενόησεν γὰρ ἑαυτὸν καὶ ἀπελήλυθεν, καὶ εὐθέως ἐπελάθετο ὁποῖος ἦν. **25** Ὁ δὲ παρακύψας εἰς νόμον τέλειον τὸν τῆς ἐλευθερίας καὶ παραμείνας, οὗτος οὐκ ἀκροατὴς ἐπιλησμονῆς γενόμενος ἀλλὰ ποιητὴς ἔργου, οὗτος μακάριος ἐν τῇ ποιήσει αὐτοῦ ἔσται. **26** Εἴ τις δοκεῖ θρῆσκος εἶναι ἐν ὑμῖν, μὴ χαλιναγωγῶν γλῶσσαν αὐτοῦ, ἀλλὰ ἀπατῶν καρδίαν αὐτοῦ, τούτου μάταιος ἡ θρησκεία. **27** Θρησκεία καθαρὰ καὶ ἀμίαντος παρὰ θεῷ καὶ πατρὶ αὕτη ἐστίν, ἐπισκέπτεσθαι ὀρφανοὺς καὶ χήρας ἐν τῇ θλίψει αὐτῶν, ἄσπιλον ἑαυτὸν τηρεῖν ἀπὸ τοῦ κόσμου.

Language

    Process of Discovery

      Linguistics Section

      Linguistic Structure

[Greeting] 1   [1a]James, a [b]bond-servant of God and [c]of the Lord Jesus Christ, to [d]the twelve tribes who are [2e]dispersed abroad: [f]Greetings. **2**   [a]Consider it all joy, my brethren, when you encounter [b]various [1]trials, **3** knowing that [a]the testing of your [b]faith produces [1c]endurance. **4** And let [1a]endurance have *its* perfect [2]result, so that you may be [3b]perfect and complete, lacking in nothing. **5**   But if any of you [a]lacks wisdom, let him ask of God, who gives to all generously and [1]without reproach, and [b]it will be given to him. **6** But he must [a]ask in faith [b]without any doubting, for the one who doubts is like the surf of the sea, [c]driven and tossed by the wind. **7** For that man ought not to expect that he will receive anything from the Lord, **8** *being* a [1a]double-minded man, [b]unstable in all his ways. **9**   [a]But the [1]brother of humble circumstances is to glory in his high position; **10** and the rich man *is to glory* in his humiliation, because [a]like [1]flowering grass he will pass away. **11** For the sun rises with [1a]a scorching wind and [b]withers the grass; and its flower falls off and the beauty of its appearance is destroyed; so too the rich man in the midst of his pursuits will fade away.

[Beattitude]12   [a]Blessed is a man who perseveres under trial; for once he has [1]been approved, he will receive [b]the crown of life which *the Lord* [c]has promised to those who [d]love Him.

[Command] 13 Let no one say when he is tempted, "[a]I am being tempted [1]by God"; for God cannot be tempted [2]by evil, and He Himself does not tempt anyone.

[Warning] 14 But each one is tempted when he is carried away and enticed by his own lust. **15** Then [a]when lust has conceived, it gives birth to sin; and when [b]sin [1]is accomplished, it brings forth death. **16** [a]Do not be [1]deceived, [b]my beloved brethren. **17** Every good thing given and every perfect gift is [a]from above, coming down from [b]the Father of lights, [c]with whom there is no variation or [1]shifting shadow. **18** In the exercise of [a]His will He [b]brought us forth by [c]the word of truth, so that we would be [1a]a kind of [d]first fruits [2]among His creatures.

A 1:19   [1]*This* [a]you know, [b]my beloved brethren. But everyone must be quick to hear, [c]slow to speak *and* [d]slow to anger; **20** for [a]the anger of man does not achieve the righteousness of God.

B 21 Therefore, *a*putting aside all filthiness and *all* [1]that remains of wickedness, in [2]humility receive *b*the word implanted, which is able to save your souls. **22** *a*But prove yourselves doers of the word, and not merely hearers who delude themselves.

> **C 23** For if anyone is a hearer of the word and not a doer, he is like a man who looks at his [1]natural face *a*in a mirror; **24** for *once* he has looked at himself and gone away, [1]he has immediately forgotten what kind of person he was.

B' 25 But one who looks intently at the perfect law, *a*the *law* of liberty, and abides by it, not having become a forgetful hearer but [1]an effectual doer, this man will be *b*blessed in [2]what he does.

A' 1:26 If anyone thinks himself to be religious, and yet does not [1a]bridle his tongue but deceives his *own* heart, this man's religion is worthless. **27** Pure and undefiled religion *a*in the sight of *our* God and Father is this: to *b*visit *c*orphans and widows in their distress, *and* to keep oneself unstained [1]by *d*the world.

Discussion

This chapter contains one chiasm at the end of the chapter. Beatitudes, commands, and warnings follow the greeting.

Questioning the Passage

1. Who are the twelve tribes who are dispersed abroad? (v. 1)

    When the Babylonians invaded Judea, they took the Judeans into exile. When the Persians took over the Babylonian empire, they allowed the Jews to return to Judea. Many of them did not want to return and stayed in Babylon. When the Assyrians invaded the northern kingdom, they transplanted the ten tribes into various parts of their empire. This became known as the diaspora. This letter from James was written to all the tribes in the diaspora. This raises the question of when it was written. There were Jews in Judea until 135 CE, when the Romans kicked them out of that territory.

2. How many places did the letter get sent to? (v. 1)
    The Letter of James in the New Testament is addressed to the "twelve tribes in the dispersion." This phrase is understood to mean Jewish Christians scattered outside of Palestine. It does not specify a certain number of churches. Instead, it suggests that the letter was intended for a broad audience of believers, potentially encompassing multiple churches. The exact number of churches that received James' letter is not specified in the biblical text.

3. What is a bond-servant of God? (v. 1)
    A bondservant of God is a person who only does God's work.

4. What are the various trials? (v. 2)
    The author is referring to temptations of the material world that often cause the faithful to depart from God's way.[5]

5. How does the testing of faith produce endurance? (v. 3)
    It was believed that temptations of the material world help disciples to gain a better understanding of life and its purpose. They could share their experiences with others, and it was believed that it would strengthen their faith. They would put aside their material wants and needs and work for God alone.

---

[5] 1. Rocco A. Errico and George M. Lamsa, *Aramaic Light on James through Revelation: A Commentary Based on Aramaic, the Language of Jesus, and Ancient near Eastern Customs* (Smyma, GA: Noohra Foundation, 2006).

6. What is the perfect work? (v. 4)

Perfect work is when a person remains consistent through opposition or continues despite the difficulty. The "perfect work" of patience results in three ends: "perfect," "complete," and "lack nothing." This is the full effect of the principle of perseverance working in our lives. The word "work" shows that perseverance is not passive, but active. A heavy trial should not daunt or defeat us.

We should rejoice in the trials, count it all as joy. Not because we enjoy the pain, but because we know what trials will produce. The "perfect work" in James 1:4 refers to the spiritual maturity and completeness that comes from enduring trials with steadfast faith.[6]

7. What does it mean to be complete (mature)? (v. 4)

The author is referring to a completeness of spirituality. It means coming to a full understanding of Yeshua as God's Messiah.

8. What does "lacking in nothing" mean? (v. 4)

This term means that there would be nothing missing from one's understanding of Yeshua as God's Messiah. Everything that we need to know as human beings about how God's Messiah and his salvation works will be given to us. That may require faith and not a full scientific understanding.

---

[6] 1. Jeffery Curtis Poor and Follow MeJeffery Curtis PoorHusband. Father. Pastor. Church Planter. Writer. Trying to be more like Jesus each day. BA in Biblical Studies - Ozark Christian College (2012) MA in Theology - Regent University (2019) Email Me: Email, "The Powerful Meaning of James 1:2-4 (Count It All Joy)," Rethink, October 19, 2023, https://www.rethinknow.org/meaning-of-james-1-2-4-count-it-all-joy/.

9. What does it mean to ask in faith? (v. 6)

This is when one asks for God's help to accomplish a task. It also infers that we trust God to give us the correct answer.

10. What does verse nine mean?

In this verse, James is addressing believers who are of low social or economic status.

"Let the lowly brother" refers to a Christian who is poor or of low social status. James is speaking to those who are humble or undistinguished in society.

"Boast in his exaltation" suggests that these lowly brothers should take pride or rejoice in their spiritual status. Despite their lowly circumstances, they have been exalted through their faith in Christ. They are children of God, heirs of the kingdom, and possessors of eternal life.

This verse encourages believers of low degree to rejoice in their spiritual exaltation. Despite their humble circumstances, they have been honored and exalted through their faith in Christ.[7]

11. What does verse ten mean?

In this verse, James is addressing believers who are rich.

"But the rich" refers to a Christian who is rich or of high social status. James is speaking to those who are distinguished in society.

---

[7] 1. "James 1:9," BibleRef.com, accessed April 29, 2024, https://www.bibleref.com/James/1/James-1-9.html.

"In that he is made low" suggests that the rich should take pride in their humiliation. Despite their high status, they are reminded of their mortality and the transient nature of earthly riches.

"Because as the flower of the grass he shall pass away" is a metaphor illustrating the fleeting nature of life and earthly riches. Just as a flower of the field blooms and then withers, so too will the rich person pass away.[8]

This verse teaches that earthly riches and status are temporary. It encourages rich believers to humble themselves and to remember the transient nature of life and earthly wealth.[9]

12. What does verse eleven mean?

In this verse, James continues his discussion about the fleeting nature of earthly riches that he started in the previous verse.

"For the sun rises with a scorching wind and withers the grass; its flower falls off and the beauty of its appearance is destroyed" is a metaphor illustrating the transient nature of life and earthly riches. Just as a flower of the field blooms and then withers under the scorching sun, so too will the rich person's life and wealth fade away.

"So also the rich person, in the midst of his pursuits, will die out" suggests that the rich person, despite all their pursuits and achievements, will eventually pass away just like everyone else. Their wealth cannot prevent the inevitable outcome of mortality.

---

[8] 1. James 1:10 commentaries: And the rich man is to glory in his humiliation, because like flowering grass he will pass away., accessed April 29, 2024, https://biblehub.com/commentaries/james/1-10.htm.

[9] 1. "James 1:10," BibleRef.com, accessed April 29, 2024, https://www.bibleref.com/James/1/James-1-10.html.

In summary, James 1:11 teaches that earthly riches and status are temporary. It encourages rich believers to remember the transient nature of life and earthly wealth.[10]

13. What does the beatitude mean? (v. 12)

The verse is essentially a message of encouragement and promise.

"Blessed is the man who perseveres under trial" is encouraging believers to remain steadfast and endure through trials and tribulations.

"When he has stood the test" implies that trials are tests of faith, and those who stand firm during these tests show their faith and commitment to God.

"He will receive the crown of life that God has promised to those who love him." This is the promise that those who endure trials and remain faithful to God will receive the "crown of life". This is not a physical crown, but a metaphor for eternal life or salvation. It has a reward not only for the distant future but also for the here and now.[11]

14. Does verse thirteen contradict the "Lord's Prayer" about temptation? (v. 13)

Many Near Eastern religions attribute everything that happens in one's life to God. It is God who tries people to test their strength and faith. Temptations and mishaps in life are blamed on God. Therefore, asking God to keep one away from temptation as is done in the LORD's prayer fits the culture.[12]

---

[10] 1. "What Does James 1:11 Mean?," Verse of the day, accessed April 29, 2024, https://dailyverse.knowing-jesus.com/james-1-11.

[11] 1. GotQuestions.org, "Home," GotQuestions.org, March 16, 2022, https://www.gotquestions.org/blessed-is-the-man-who-perseveres-under-trial.html.

[12] 1. Rocco A. Errico and George M. Lamsa, *Aramaic Light on James through Revelation: A Commentary Based on Aramaic, the Language of Jesus, and Ancient near Eastern Customs* (Smyrna, GA: Noohra Foundation, 2006).

15. What does verse fifteen mean? (v. 15)

Any form of lust, if allowed to continue within a person, will eventually drive them into sinning because they want to fulfill the lust. It is also believed that unforgiven sin leads to death.

16. What is a perfect gift? (v. 17)

The perfect gift is any gift that God sends to humanity. Perfect gives help humanity to grow both physically and spiritually.

17. Who is the "Father of lights?" (v. 17)

God is the Father of lights. It is a near Eastern expression which reminds us that God is the creator of light. God created visible light but also God's light is God's power which sustains the universe.

18. What does it mean to be the first fruits among His creatures? (v. 18)

"He chose to give us birth through the word of truth" suggests that God, by His own will, gave us new life or "birth" through the "word of truth", which is often interpreted as the gospel or the message of Jesus Christ.

"That we might be a kind of firstfruits of all he created." The term "firstfruits" was familiar to the Jewish audience of James' epistle. It refers to the first portion of the harvest that was given to God as an offering of gratitude.

Firstfruits of salvation: The first-century believers were the first to be saved and be part of the New Testament church. The term implies that there would be many more believers to come.

Firstfruits of the new creation: Believers are new creations in Christ. When God saves us and gives us eternal life, He cancels out the curse of sin in our lives. This change in the believer is a sign of a bigger change coming, because God will one day cancel out the curse of sin on all of creation.

James 1:18 is a verse that describes believers as the "firstfruits" of God's creation, emphasizing that they have been given new life through the "word of truth."[13]

19. What does "begat us by the word of truth" in verse eighteen mean?
This means that through the word of God, which is the word of truth, God allows us to be reborn through Yeshua, thus receiving forgiveness for sin and the hope of eternal salvation.

20. What were the impurities of James' time? (v. 21)
The author wrote this letter to Jewish followers of Yeshua. These Jews were still loyal to their faith and the ordinances and rituals. They had a difficult time leaving them behind. James hoped that the gospel of Yeshua would be grafted into their psyche and thus would remove the ancient faith from them. The impurities that he is referring to are the ancient ways of Judaism.

21. What is the perfect law in verse twenty-five?
The author is referring to the Gospels of Yeshua as the perfect law.

22. What is the law of liberty? (v. 25)
This is another way of saying the gospel of Yeshua.

---

[13] 1. GotQuestions.org, "Home," GotQuestions.org, June 13, 2022, https://www.gotquestions.org/firstfruits-of-His-creatures.html.

23. How does one deceive one's heart? (v. 26)

This refers to people who profess a religion but do not follow what the religion says.

24. What does it mean to keep oneself unstained (unspotted) by the world? (v. 27)

This statement means that one should not be influenced by materialism of the world but by the spirituality of faith in Yeshua and God.

Biblical Personalities

1. James – the author of this epistle and an apostle of Yeshua.

Thoughts

James did not like rich people, period. He was very clear about this thought. There is nothing wrong with having wealth. It is what one does with their wealth that matters.

Chapter Two

Language

Peshitta	New American Standard 1995
2:1 My brethren, hold ye not the faith of the glory of our Lord Jesus the Messiah, with a respect to persons. **2** For if there come into your assembly a man with rings of gold or splendid garments, and there come in a poor man in sordid garments; **3** and ye show respect to him who is clothed in splendid garments, and say to him, Seat thyself here, conspicuously; while to the poor man, ye say, Stand thou there, or sit thou here before my footstool; **4** are ye not divided among yourselves, and become expositors of evil thoughts? **5** Hear, my beloved brethren; hath not God chosen the poor of the world, but the rich in faith, to be heirs in the kingdom which God hath promised to them that love him? **6** But ye have despised the poor man. Do not rich men exalt themselves over you, and drag you before the tribunals? **7** Do they not revile that worthy name, which is invoked upon you? **8** And if in this ye fulfill the law of God, as it is written, Thou shalt love thy neighbor as thyself, ye will do well: **9** but if ye have respect of persons, ye commit sin; and ye are convicted by the law, as transgressors of the law. **10** For he that shall keep the whole law, and yet fail in one [precept], is obnoxious to the whole law. **11** For he who said, Thou shalt not commit adultery, said also, Thou shalt not kill. If then thou commit no adultery, but thou killest, thou hast become a transgressor of the law. **12** So speak ye, and	**James 2:1** [a]My brethren, [b]do not hold your faith in our [c]glorious Lord Jesus Christ with *an attitude of* [d]personal favoritism. **2** For if a man comes into your [1]assembly with a gold ring and dressed in [2a]fine clothes, and there also comes in a poor man in [b]dirty clothes, **3** and you [1]pay special attention to the one who is wearing the [a]fine clothes, and say, "You sit here in a good place," and you say to the poor man, "You stand over there, or sit down by my footstool," **4** have you not made distinctions among yourselves, and become judges [a]with evil [1]motives? **5** Listen, [a]my beloved brethren: did not [b]God choose the poor [1]of this world *to be* [c]rich in faith and [d]heirs of the kingdom which He [e]promised to those who love Him? **6** But you have dishonored the poor man. Is it not the rich who oppress you and [1]personally [a]drag you into [2]court? **7** [a]Do they not blaspheme the fair name [1]by which you have been called? **James 2:8** If, however, you [a]are fulfilling the [1]royal law according to the Scripture, "[b]YOU SHALL LOVE YOUR NEIGHBOR AS YOURSELF," you are doing well. **9** But if you [a]show partiality, you are committing sin *and* are convicted by the [1]law as transgressors. **10** For whoever keeps the whole [1]law and yet [a]stumbles in one *point,* he has become [b]guilty of all. **11** For He who says, "[a]DO

so act, as persons that are to be judged by the law of liberty. **13** For judgment without mercy shall be on him, who hath practised no mercy: by mercy, ye will be raised above judgment. **14** What is the use, my brethren, if a man say, I have faith; and he hath no works? can his faith vivify him? **15** Or if a brother or sister be naked, and destitute of daily food, **16** and one of you say to them, Go in peace, warm yourselves, and be full; and ye give them not the necessaries of the body, what is the use? **17** So also faith alone, without works, is dead. **18** For a man may say, Thou hast faith, and I have works; show to me thy faith that is without works; and I will show to thee, my faith by my works. **19** Thou believest that there is one God; thou dost well; the demons also believe, and tremble. **20** Wouldst thou know, O frail man, that faith without works is dead? **21** Abraham our father, was not he justified by works, in offering his son Isaac upon the altar? **22** Seest thou, that his faith aided his works; and that by the works his faith was rendered complete? **23** And the scripture was fulfilled, which saith: Abraham believed in God, and it was accounted to him for righteousness, and he was called the Friend of God. **24** Thou seest, that by works a man is justified, and not by faith alone. **25** So also Rahab, the harlot, was not she justified by works, when she entertained the spies, and sent them forth by another way? **26** As the body without the spirit, is dead; so faith without works, is dead also.

NOT COMMIT ADULTERY," also says, "[b]DO NOT COMMIT MURDER." Now if you do not commit adultery, but do commit murder, you have become a transgressor of the [1]law. **12** So speak and so act as those who are to be judged by [a]*the* law of liberty. **13** For [a]judgment *will be* merciless to one who has shown no mercy; mercy [1]triumphs over judgment.

Faith and Works

James 2:14 [a]What use is it, [b]my brethren, if someone says he has faith but he has no works? Can [1]that faith save him? **15** [a]If a brother or sister is without clothing and in need of daily food, **16** and one of you says to them, "[a]Go in peace, [1]be warmed and be filled," and yet you do not give them what is necessary for *their* body, what use is that? **17** Even so [a]faith, if it has no works, is [1]dead, *being* by itself.

James 2:18 [a]But someone [1]may *well* say, "You have faith and I have works; show me your [b]faith without the works, and I will [c]show you my faith [d]by my works." **19** You believe that [1a]God is one. [b]You do well; [c]the demons also believe, and shudder. **20** But are you willing to recognize, [a]you foolish fellow, that [b]faith without works is useless? **21** [a]Was not Abraham our father justified by works when he offered up Isaac his son on the altar? **22** You see that [a]faith was working with his works, and [1]as a result of the [b]works, faith was [2]perfected; **23** and the Scripture was fulfilled which says, "[a]AND ABRAHAM BELIEVED GOD, AND IT WAS RECKONED TO HIM AS RIGHTEOUSNESS," and he was called

<table>
<tr><td></td><td>^bthe friend of God. ²⁴ You see that a man is justified by works and not by faith alone. ²⁵ In the same way, was not ^aRahab the harlot also justified by works ^bwhen she received the messengers and sent them out by another way? ²⁶ For just as the body without *the* spirit is dead, so also ^afaith without works is dead.</td></tr>
</table>

References to the New American Standard 1995

James 2:1
^aJames 1:16
^bHeb 12:2
^cActs 7:2; 1 Cor 2:8
^dActs 10:34; James 2:9

James 2:2
¹Or *synagogue*
²Or *bright*
^aLuke 23:11; James 2:3
^bZech 3:3f

James 2:3
¹Lit *look at*
^aLuke 23:11

James 2:4
¹Lit *reasonings*
^aLuke 18:6; John 7:24

James 2:5
¹Lit *to the*
^aJames 1:16
^bJob 34:19; 1 Cor 1:27f

[c]Luke 12:21; Rev 2:9
[d]Matt 5:3; 25:34
[e]James 1:12

James 2:6
[1]Lit *they themselves*
[2]Lit *courts*
[a]Acts 8:3; 16:19

James 2:7
[1]Lit *which has been called upon you*
[a]Acts 11:26; 1 Pet 4:16

James 2:8
[1]Or *law of our King*
[a]Matt 7:12
[b]Lev 19:18

James 2:9
[1]Or *Law*
[a]Acts 10:34; James 2:1

James 2:10
[1]Or *Law*
[a]James 3:2; 2 Pet 1:10; Jude 24
[b]Matt 5:19; Gal 5:3

James 2:11
[1]Or *Law*
[a]Ex 20:14; Deut 5:18
[b]Ex 20:13; Deut 5:17

James 2:12
[a]James 1:25

James 2:13
[1]Lit *boasts against*
[a]Prov 21:13; Matt 5:7; 18:32-35; Luke 6:37f

James 2:14
[1]Lit *the*

[a]James 1:22ff
[b]James 1:16

James 2:15
[a]Matt 25:35f; Luke 3:11

James 2:16
[1]Or *warm yourselves and fill yourselves*
[a]1 John 3:17f

James 2:17
[1]Or *dead by its own standards*
[a]Gal 5:6; James 2:20, 26

James 2:18
[1]Lit *will*
[a]Rom 9:19
[b]Rom 3:28; 4:6; Heb 11:33
[c]James 3:13
[d]Matt 7:16f; Gal 5:6

James 2:19
[1]One early ms reads *there is one God*
[a]Deut 6:4; Mark 12:29
[b]James 2:8
[c]Matt 8:29; Mark 1:24; 5:7; Luke 4:34; Acts 19:15

James 2:20
[a]Rom 9:20; 1 Cor 15:36
[b]Gal 5:6; James 2:17, 26

James 2:21
[a]Gen 22:9, 10, 12, 16-18

James 2:22
[1]Or *by the deeds*
[2]Or *completed*
[a]John 6:29; Heb 11:17
[b]1 Thess 1:3

James 2:23

[a]Gen 15:6; Rom 4:3
[b]2 Chr 20:7; Is 41:8

James 2:25
[a]Heb 11:31
[b]Josh 2:4, 6, 15

James 2:26
[a]Gal 5:6; James 2:17, 20

Koine Greek

James 2:1 Αδελφοι μου, μη εν προσωπολημψιαις εχετε την πιστιν του κυριου ημων Ιησου Χριστου της δοξης. ² εαν γαρ εισελθη εις συναγωγην υμων ανηρ χρυσοδακτυλιος εν εσθητι λαμπρα, εισελθη δε και πτωχος εν ρυπαρα εσθητι, ³ επιβλεψητε δε επι τον φορουντα την εσθητα την λαμπραν και ειπητε· συ καθου ωδε καλως, και τω πτωχω ειπητε· συ στηθι η καθου εκει υπο το υποποδιον μου, ⁴ και ου διεκριθητε εν εαυτοις και εγενεσθε κριται διαλογισμων πονηρων; ⁵ ακουσατε, αδελφοι μου αγαπητοι· ουχ ο θεος εξελεξατο τους πτωχους τω κοσμω πλουσιους εν πιστει και κληρονομους της βασιλειας ης επηγγειλατο τοις αγαπωσιν αυτον; ⁶ υμεις δε ητιμασατε τον πτωχον. ουχ οι πλουσιοι καταδυναστευουσιν υμων και αυτοι ελκουσιν υμας εις κριτηρια; ⁷ ουκ αυτοι βλασφημουσιν το καλον ονομα το επικληθεν εφ᾽ υμας;

James 2:8 Ει μεντοι νομον τελειτε βασιλικον κατα την γραφην· *αγαπησεις τον πλησιον σου ως σεαυτον,* καλως ποιειτε· ⁹ ει δε προσωπολημπτειτε, αμαρτιαν εργαζεσθε ελεγχομενοι υπο του νομου ως παραβαται. ¹⁰ οστις γαρ ολον τον νομον τηρηση, πταιση δε εν ενι, γεγονεν παντων ενοχος. ¹¹ ο γαρ ειπων· *μη μοιχευσης,* ειπεν και· *μη φονευσης·* ει δε ου μοιχευεις, φονευεις δε, γεγονας παραβατης νομου.

James 2:12 Ουτως λαλειτε και ουτως ποιειτε ως δια νομου ελευθεριας μελλοντες κρινεσθαι. ¹³ η γαρ κρισις ανελεος τω μη ποιησαντι ελεος· κατακαυχαται ελεος κρισεως.

James 2:14 Τι το οφελος, αδελφοι μου, εαν πιστιν λεγη τις εχειν, εργα δε μη εχη; μη δυναται η πιστις σωσαι αυτον; ¹⁵ εαν αδελφος η αδελφη γυμνοι υπαρχωσιν και λειπομενοι ωσιν της εφημερου τροφης, ¹⁶ ειπη δε τις αυτοις εξ υμων· υπαγετε εν ειρηνη, θερμαινεσθε και χορταζεσθε, μη δωτε δε αυτοις τα επιτηδεια του σωματος, τι το οφελος; ¹⁷ ουτως και η πιστις, εαν μη εχη εργα, νεκρα εστιν καθ᾽ εαυτην.

James 2:18 Αλλ᾽ ερει τις· συ πιστιν εχεις, καγω εργα εχω. δειξον μοι την πιστιν σου χωρις των εργων, καγω σοι δειξω εκ των εργων μου την πιστιν. ¹⁹ συ πιστευεις οτι εις εστιν ο θεος, καλως ποιεις· και τα δαιμονια πιστευουσιν και φρισσουσιν.

James 2:20 Θελεις δε γνωναι, ω ανθρωπε κενε, οτι η πιστις χωρις των εργων αργη εστιν; ²¹ Αβρααμ ο πατηρ ημων ουκ εξ εργων εδικαιωθη ανενεγκας Ισαακ τον υιον αυτου επι το θυσιαστηριον; ²² βλεπεις οτι η πιστις συνηργει τοις εργοις αυτου και εκ των εργων η πιστις ετελειωθη, ²³ και επληρωθη η γραφη η λεγουσα· *επιστευσεν δε Αβρααμ τω θεω, και ελογισθη αυτω εις δικαιοσυνην* και φιλος θεου εκληθη. ²⁴ ορατε οτι εξ εργων δικαιουται ανθρωπος και ουκ εκ πιστεως μονον. ²⁵ ομοιως δε και Ρααβ η πορνη ουκ εξ εργων εδικαιωθη υποδεξαμενη τους αγγελους και ετερα οδω εκβαλουσα; ²⁶ ωσπερ γαρ το σωμα χωρις πνευματος νεκρον εστιν, ουτως και η πιστις χωρις εργων νεκρα εστιν.

Language

  Process of Discovery

    Linguistics Section

      Linguistic Structure

[Rich People] 1 *a*My brethren, *b*do not hold your faith in our *c*glorious Lord Jesus Christ with *an attitude of* *d*personal favoritism. **2** For if a man comes into your [1]assembly with a gold ring and dressed in [2a]fine clothes, and there also comes in a poor man in *b*dirty clothes, **3** and you [1]pay special attention to the one who is wearing the *a*fine clothes, and say, "You sit here in a good place," and you say to the poor man, "You stand over there, or sit down by my footstool," **4** have you not made distinctions among yourselves, and become judges *a*with evil [1]motives? **5** Listen, *a*my beloved brethren: did not *b*God choose the poor [1]of this world *to be* *c*rich in faith and *d*heirs of the kingdom which He *e*promised to those who love Him? **6** But you have dishonored the poor man. Is it not the rich who oppress you and [1]personally *a*drag you into [2]court? **7** *a*Do they not blaspheme the fair name [1]by which you have been called?

[Royal Law] 8 If, however, you *a*are fulfilling the [1]royal law according to the Scripture, "*b*YOU SHALL LOVE YOUR NEIGHBOR AS YOURSELF," you are doing well. **9** But if you *a*show partiality, you are committing sin *and* are convicted by the [1]law as transgressors. **10** For whoever keeps the whole [1]law and yet *a*stumbles in one *point,* he has become *b*guilty of all. **11** For He who said, "*a*DO NOT COMMIT ADULTERY," also said, "*b*DO NOT COMMIT MURDER." Now if you do not commit adultery, but do commit murder, you have become a transgressor of the [1]law. **12** So speak and so act as those who are to be judged by *a*the law of liberty. **13** For *a*judgment *will be* merciless to one who has shown no mercy; mercy [1]triumphs over judgment.

[Faith and works] 14 *a*What use is it, *b*my brethren, if someone says he has faith but he has no works? Can [1]that faith save him? **15** *a*If a brother or sister is without clothing and in need of daily food, **16** and one of you says to them, "*a*Go in peace, [1]be warmed and be filled," and yet you do not give them what is necessary for *their* body, what use is that? **17** Even so *a*faith, if it has no works, is [1]dead, *being* by itself. **18** *a*But someone

[1]may *well* say, "You have faith and I have works; show me your [b]faith without the works, and I will [c]show you my faith [d]by my works." **19** You believe that [1a]God is one. [b]You do well; [c]the demons also believe, and shudder. **20** But are you willing to recognize, [a]you foolish fellow, that [b]faith without works is useless? **21** [a]Was not Abraham our father justified by works when he offered up Isaac his son on the altar? **22** You see that [a]faith was working with his works, and [1]as a result of the [b]works, faith was [2]perfected; **23** and the Scripture was fulfilled which says, "[a]AND ABRAHAM BELIEVED GOD, AND IT WAS RECKONED TO HIM AS RIGHTEOUSNESS," and he was called [b]the friend of God. **24** You see that a man is justified by works and not by faith alone. **25** In the same way, was not [a]Rahab the harlot also justified by works [b]when she received the messengers and sent them out by another way? **26** For just as the body without *the* spirit is dead, so also [a]faith without works is dead.

Discussion

This chapter deals with James's opinion of rich people and faith.

Questioning the Passage

1. Is verse five a rewording of Yeshua's beatitude toward the poor? (v. 5)

   This verse shares a similar theme with the Beatitudes, specifically with Matthew 5:3, which says, "Blessed are the poor in spirit, for theirs is the kingdom of heaven." Both verses speak about the spiritual blessings promised to those who are humble or "poor" in a spiritual sense[1].

   However, James 2:5 is not a direct rewording of the Beatitudes. While both passages share common themes of humility, faith, and the promise of the kingdom of heaven, they each have their unique context and emphasis. The Book of James focuses more on the importance of faith showed through action, while the Beatitudes in the Sermon on the Mount are more about the attitudes that followers of Jesus should embody[12]. So, while there are similarities, each passage has its unique message and context.

2. Can the church have rich people? (v. 6)

   The church certainly can have rich people. The church today should apply this chapter in the sense that rich people should not get special treatment just because they are rich. Usually, what the church discovers is that a rich person likes to control the church but does not give a full tithe to the church. If the church allows a rich person or a high tithing person to control the church, then their money is being given for control and power and not for the betterment of spreading the gospel.

3. Why did rich people oppress the poor? (v. 6)

   Rich people oppress the poor because there was a zero-growth economy in place. That meant for someone to become rich, they had to take wealth away from another individual. Rich people were given high positions in government, like tax collectors, who could take from the rich and keep it for themselves.

4. What is the name invoked upon the people? (v. 7)

   The worthy name mentioned in verse seven is the name Yeshua.

5. What is a royal law? (v. 8)

   The royal law refers to the two great Commandments that Yeshua gave: love God and love neighbor.

6. What does it mean to be transgressors of the law? (v. 9)

   According to the author, a transgressor of the law is one who does not follow the royal law, which are the two great Commandments that Yeshua gave us.

7. What is the whole law? (v. 10)

The term "whole law" refers to the entirety of God's law as a unified whole. The verse emphasizes that if someone keeps the entire law but fails in one aspect, they are guilty of breaking all of it. This illustrates the principle that God's law is an integrated system, and violating any single part is akin to violating the entire law. The verse serves as a reminder of the need for mercy and grace, as no one can perfectly keep the whole law except Yeshua.[14]

8. What is the law of liberty? (v. 12)

The author is referring to the Gospels of Yeshua.

9. Do you have to show mercy to everybody to obtain mercy? (v. 13)

The author shows that if one wishes to have mercy from the Lord because of their sin that they need to show mercy to their neighbors and family.

10. What does verse fourteen through seventeen mean?

This passage emphasizes the relationship between faith and actions. The value of a faith that is not accompanied by action is questioned. It challenges the authenticity of such faith. These verses provide a practical example of the previous point. They illustrate the emptiness of words that are not backed up by actions. This section concludes the argument by stating that faith without works is dead. It emphasizes that genuine faith should manifest in tangible actions. It serves as a powerful reminder of the interconnectedness of faith and deeds. It challenges believers to examine the authenticity of their faith, emphasizing that genuine faith

---

[14] 1. "James 2:10," BibleRef.com, accessed May 11, 2024, https://www.bibleref.com/James/2/James-2-10.html.

is not merely an intellectual acknowledgment but should manifest in tangible actions.[15]

11. What does verse eighteen mean?

The author is asking can you separate faith and works. Can a person just do works, good things for the Lord, and still not have faith? Also, can a person who has faith in the Lord do nothing to show that faith?

12. What does "God is one" mean? (v. 19)

Since the idea Trinity has not been introduced yet to this author, he is following the understanding of monotheism as defined by Judaism. Polytheism was the normal for religions in the Roman Empire except for Judaism. If the author was speaking to a community of Jews, then he's just reminding them they believe in one God who created heaven and earth and sent the Messiah to be with them.

13. How was Abraham justified by works when he offered Isaac? (v. 21)

James is pointing to Abraham's faith as the motivating power behind his works. He showed it was Abraham's belief that allowed him to be counted as righteous. His works were evidence of that faith and, therefore, evidence of his salvation.

14. What is works righteousness? (v. 25)

Works righteousness is defined as the things you do to show your faith in Yeshua in order to receive that salvation that he offers.

---

[15] 1. Bob Wilkin, "Faith without Works Is Dead - James 2:14-17," Grace Evangelical Society, June 30, 2017, https://faithalone.org/blog/faith-without-works-is-dead/.

15. How does Rahab fit into works righteousness? (v. 25)

In the Near East, moral laws were strongly enforced, and the guilty were severely punished. However, harlots could be found in many of the large cities. Houses of prostitution was prohibited, therefore harlots had to work in secret. They knew who visitors to the city were. Rahab knew that the two spies that Joshua sent into the city of Jericho were strangers, and she helped them. The author believes that by Rahab helping the two spies; she received righteousness from her works. Therefore, one could say that a sinner can be turned into a righteous person by doing something important for God.

16. How was it determined that the body was dead without the spirit? (v. 26)

In this verse, the spirit refers to the soul that lives in the body. When the soul leaves the body, the body is dead. The author is comparing this to a person who says they have faith, but they do not do any good works; they do not have faith.

17. Why do you have to do work in order to have faith?

Doing good works for God shows one's faith. Think about faith as an action verb. It is easy to say that you have faith in God and Yeshua, but it is showing your faith that is important.

18. What does dead faith look like?

Dead faith is where a person claims to have faith in God and in Yeshua, but does absolutely nothing to show physically that faith.

19. Does faith have to be shown through a religious group?

Being a part of a religious group who worship Yeshua, like a church is one way to show good works. However, it is unnecessary that an individual be part of a religious group, the church, in order to have faith and to show God by works that the faith is genuine in Yeshua.

Verse Comparison of citations or proof text

1. [8] If, however, you [a]are fulfilling the [1]royal law according to the Scripture, "[b]YOU SHALL LOVE YOUR NEIGHBOR AS YOURSELF," you are doing well.

   Leviticus 19:18 'You shall not take vengeance, nor bear any grudge against the sons of your people, but you shall love your neighbor as yourself; I am the LORD.

2. [11] For He who says, "[a]DO NOT COMMIT ADULTERY," also says, "[b]DO NOT COMMIT MURDER." Now if you do not commit adultery, but do commit murder, you have become a transgressor of the [1]law.

   Exodus 20:14 "You shall not commit adultery.

3. [23] and the Scripture was fulfilled which says, "[a]AND ABRAHAM BELIEVED GOD, AND IT WAS RECKONED TO HIM AS RIGHTEOUSNESS," and he was called [b]the friend of God.

   Genesis 15:6 Then he believed in the LORD; and He reckoned it to him as righteousness.

Translation Inconsistencies

1. **James 2:1** My brethren, hold ye not the faith of the glory of our Lord Jesus the Messiah, with a respect to persons. (Peshitta)

    James 2:1 [a]My brethren, [b]do not hold your faith in our [c]glorious Lord Jesus Christ with *an attitude of* [d]personal favoritism. (NASB)

    James 2:1 My brothers and sisters,[a] do you with your acts of favoritism really believe in our glorious Lord Jesus Christ? (NRSV)

    The NRSV version is quite interesting because it places a question about favoritism in that if you show favoritism, do you believe in Yeshua?

Culture Section

Discussion

In many of the cities and provinces in the Near East, the government was controlled by rich people. Most of the civil positions, like judges, were gained by bribes and promises of good revenue. In return, the government gave these people unlimited power. Tax collectors would not tax rich people because they were concerned about retribution. Wealthy people who gained their wealth by the hand of God and not by exploitation should not be considered members of this group of rich people the author disliked. People need to learn to be content with the labor of their own hands and satisfied with whatever God gives them.

The author did not like rich people, period. He was very clear about this thought. There is nothing wrong with having wealth. It is what one does with their wealth that matters. Clothing was scarce and in James' day and quite expensive. Only rich people could afford to have expensive garments and precious jewels. During weddings and special occasions, people wore numerous garments so that they could receive respect and admiration from the other guests at the occasion. A man might not have sufficient clothes to attend such a gathering so he would have to borrow clothing from a friend or neighbor. People who were dressed poorly were given less important places and received little attention. James in this letter condemns this ancient practice and believed that a person should be judged on their character and demeanor and not by their clothing.[16]

This book puts a heavy emphasis on sharing, giving, and good works. The author made the point in this chapter to say that faith without works is dead. How do you prove to God that you believe in him if you lead an evil life?

Historical Notes

In the Middle Ages, the term for church apathy was "acedia". Acedia (also known as accidie) originated from the Greek word ἀκηδία, which conveyed a state of listlessness, torpor, or indifference. In ancient Greece, it referred to an inert condition devoid of pain or care. Early Christian monks adopted this term to describe a spiritual state of listlessness. Over time, it gained a distinctly Christian moral tone. Acedia was one of the eight genera of evil thoughts by Evagrius of Pontus. It manifested as a temptation—a restlessness that hindered work and prayer. The noonday demon was another name for acedia, as depicted by the Desert Father John Cassian. It led to unreasonable confusion and a sense of darkness.

---

[16] 1. Rocco A. Errico and George M. Lamsa, *Aramaic Light on James through Revelation: A Commentary Based on Aramaic, the Language of Jesus, and Ancient near Eastern Customs* (Smyma, GA: Noohra Foundation, 2006).

In the medieval Latin tradition of the seven deadly sins, acedia was often associated with sloth and other negative states.

During the Middle Ages, people's lives revolved around the Church. Laymen and theologians alike recognized the vice of acedia, which signified a restlessness preventing both work and prayer. It was a state of inability to engage fully in spiritual practices.

Thoughts

The important point in this chapter is faith without works is dead. Faith is an action, not just something you say. Therefore, if you say that you believe in God and the salvation offered by Yeshua's life and death, then you need to show God that you believe by acting like Yeshua did.

Chapter Three

Language

Peshitta	New American Standard 1995
3:1 Let there not be many teachers among you, my brethren; but know ye, that we are obnoxious to a severer judgment. **2** For we all offend in many things. Whoever offendeth not in discourse, is a perfect man, who can also keep his whole body in subjection. **3** Behold, we put bridles into the mouth of horses, that they may obey us; and we turn about their whole body. **4** Huge ships also, when strong winds drive them, are turned about by a small timber, to what place the pleasure of the pilot looketh. **5** So likewise the tongue is a small member, and it exalteth itself. Also a little fire inflameth large forests. **6** Now the tongue is a fire, and the world of sin is like a forest. And this tongue, which is one among our members, marreth our whole body; and it inflameth the series of our generations that roll on like a wheel; and it is itself on fire. **7** For all natures of beasts and birds and reptiles, of the sea or land, are subjugated by the nature of man. **8** But the tongue hath no one been able to tame: it is an evil thing, not coercible, and full of deadly poison. **9** For with it, we bless the Lord and Father; and with it we curse men, who were made in the image of God: **10** and from the same mouth, proceed curses and blessings. My brethren, these things ought not to be so. **11** Can there flow from the same fountain, sweet waters and bitter? **12** Or can the fig-tree, my brethren, bear olives? or the vine, figs? So also salt	**3:1** *a*Let not many *of you* become teachers, *b*my brethren, knowing that as such we will incur a [1]stricter judgment. **2** For we all *a*stumble in many *ways*. *b*If anyone does not stumble in [1]what he says, he is a *c*perfect man, able to *d*bridle the whole body as well. **3** Now *a*if we put the bits into the horses' mouths so that they will obey us, we direct their entire body as well. **4** Look at the ships also, though they are so great and are driven by strong winds, are still directed by a very small rudder wherever the inclination of the pilot desires. **5** So also the tongue is a small part of the body, and *yet* it *a*boasts of great things. *b*See how great a forest is set aflame by such a small fire! **6** And *a*the tongue is a fire, the *very* world of iniquity; the tongue is set among our members as that which *b*defiles the entire body, and sets on fire the course of *our* [1]life, and is set on fire by [2c]hell. **7** For every [1]species of beasts and birds, of reptiles and creatures of the sea, is tamed and has been tamed by the human [1]race. **8** But no one can tame the tongue; *it is a* restless evil *and* full of *a*deadly poison. **9** With it we bless *a*our Lord and Father, and with it we curse men, *b*who have been made in the likeness of God; **10** from the same mouth come *both* blessing and cursing. My brethren, these things ought not to be this way. **11** Does a fountain send out from the same opening *both*

waters cannot be made sweet. **13** Who is wise and instructed among you? Let him show his works in praiseworthy actions, with modest wisdom. **14** But if bitter envy be in you, or contention in your hearts, exalt not yourselves against the truth, and lie not. **15** For this wisdom cometh not down from above; but is earthly, and from the devices of the soul, and from demons. **16** For where envy and contention are, there also is confusion, and every thing wrong. **17** But the wisdom which is from above, is pure, and full of peace, and mild, and submissive, and full of compassion and of good fruits, and without partiality, and without respect of persons. **18** And the fruits of righteousness are sown in stillness, by them who make peace.

[1]fresh and bitter *water?* **12** [a]Can a fig tree, my brethren, produce olives, or a vine produce figs? Nor *can* salt water produce [1]fresh. **13** Who among you is wise and understanding? [a]Let him show by his [b]good behavior his deeds in the gentleness of wisdom. **14** But if you have bitter [a]jealousy and [1]selfish ambition in your heart, do not be arrogant and *so* lie against [b]the truth. **15** This wisdom is not that which comes down [a]from above, but is [b]earthly, [1c]natural, [d]demonic. **16** For where [a]jealousy and [1]selfish ambition exist, [2]there is disorder and every evil thing. **17** But the wisdom [a]from above is first [b]pure, then [c]peaceable, [d]gentle, [1]reasonable, [e]full of mercy and good fruits, [f]unwavering, without [g]hypocrisy. **18** And the [1a]seed whose fruit is righteousness is sown in peace [2]by those who make peace.

James 3:1
[1]Or *greater condemnation*
[a]Matt 23:8; Rom 2:20f; 1 Tim 1:7
[b]James 1:16; 3:10

James 3:2
[1]Lit *word*
[a]James 2:10
[b]Matt 12:34-37; James 3:2-12
[c]James 1:4
[d]James 1:26

James 3:3
[a]Ps 32:9

James 3:5
[a]Ps 12:3f; 73:8f
[b]Prov 26:20f

James 3:6
[1]Or *existence, origin*
[2]Gr *Gehenna*
[a]Ps 120:2, 3; Prov 16:27
[b]Matt 12:36f; 15:11, 18f
[c]Matt 5:22

James 3:7
[1]Lit *nature*

James 3:8
[a]Ps 140:3; Eccl 10:11; Rom 3:13

James 3:9
[a]James 1:27
[b]Gen 1:26; 1 Cor 11:7

James 3:11

[1]Lit *sweet*

James 3:12
[1]V 11, note 1
[a]Matt 7:16

James 3:13
[a]James 2:18
[b]1 Pet 2:12

James 3:14
[1]Or *strife*
[a]Rom 2:8; 2 Cor 12:20; James 3:16
[b]1 Tim 2:4; James 1:18; 5:19

James 3:15
[1]Or *unspiritual*
[a]James 1:17
[b]1 Cor 2:6; 3:19
[c]2 Cor 1:12; Jude 19
[d]2 Thess 2:9f; 1 Tim 4:1; Rev 2:24

James 3:16
[1]V 14, note 1
[2]I.e. in that place
[a]Rom 2:8; 2 Cor 12:20; James 3:14

James 3:17
[1]Or *willing to yield*
[a]James 1:17
[b]2 Cor 7:11; James 4:8
[c]Matt 5:9; Heb 12:11
[d]Titus 3:2
[e]Luke 6:36; James 2:13
[f]James 2:4
[g]Rom 12:9; 2 Cor 6:6

James 3:18
[1]Lit *fruit of righteousness*
[2]Or *for*
[a]Prov 11:18; Is 32:17; Hos 10:12; Amos 6:12; Gal 6:8; Phil 1:11

3:1 Μη πολλοι διδασκαλοι γινεσθε, αδελφοι μου, ειδοτες οτι μειζον κριμα λημψομεθα. ² πολλα γαρ πταιομεν απαντες. ει τις εν λογω ου πταιει, ουτος τελειος ανηρ δυνατος χαλιναγωγησαι και ολον το σωμα. ³ ει δε των ιππων τους χαλινους εις τα στοματα βαλλομεν εις το πειθεσθαι αυτους ημιν, και ολον το σωμα αυτων μεταγομεν. ⁴ ιδου και τα πλοια τηλικαυτα οντα και υπο ανεμων σκληρων ελαυνομενα μεταγεται υπο ελαχιστου πηδαλιου οπου η ορμη του ευθυνοντος βουλεται. ⁵ ουτως και η γλωσσα μικρον μελος εστιν και μεγαλα αυχει. ιδου ηλικον πυρ ηλικην υλην αναπτει. ⁶ και η γλωσσα πυρ. ο κοσμος της αδικιας η γλωσσα καθισταται εν τοις μελεσιν ημων η σπιλουσα ολον το σωμα και φλογιζουσα τον τροχον της γενεσεως και φλογιζομενη υπο της γεεννης. ⁷ πασα γαρ φυσις θηριων τε και πετεινων, ερπετων τε και εναλιων δαμαζεται και δεδαμασται τη φυσει τη ανθρωπινη, ⁸ την δε γλωσσαν ουδεις δαμασαι δυναται ανθρωπων, ακαταστατον κακον, μεστη ιου θανατηφορου. ⁹ εν αυτη ευλογουμεν τον κυριον και πατερα και εν αυτη καταρωμεθα τους ανθρωπους τους καθ' ομοιωσιν θεου γεγονοτας· ¹⁰ εκ του αυτου στοματος εξερχεται ευλογια και καταρα. ου χρη, αδελφοι μου, ταυτα ουτως γινεσθαι. ¹¹ μητι η πηγη εκ της αυτης οπης βρυει το γλυκυ και το πικρον; ¹² μη δυναται, αδελφοι μου, συκη ελαιας ποιησαι η αμπελος συκα; ουτε αλυκον γλυκυ ποιησαι υδωρ.

3:13 Τις σοφος και επιστημων εν υμιν; δειξατω εκ της καλης αναστροφης τα εργα αυτου εν πραυτητι σοφιας. ¹⁴ ει δε ζηλον πικρον εχετε και εριθειαν εν τη καρδια υμων, μη κατακαυχασθε και ψευδεσθε κατα της αληθειας. ¹⁵ ουκ εστιν αυτη η σοφια ανωθεν κατερχομενη αλλ' επιγειος, ψυχικη, δαιμονιωδης. ¹⁶ οπου γαρ ζηλος και εριθεια, εκει ακαταστασια και παν φαυλον πραγμα. ¹⁷ η δε ανωθεν σοφια πρωτον μεν αγνη εστιν, επειτα ειρηνικη, επιεικης, ευπειθης, μεστη ελεους και καρπων αγαθων, αδιακριτος, ανυποκριτος. ¹⁸ καρπος δε δικαιοσυνης εν ειρηνη σπειρεται τοις ποιουσιν ειρηνην.

Language
  Process of Discovery

   Linguistics Section

   Linguistic Structure

[Warning about teaching] 3:1 *a*Let not many *of you* become teachers, *b*my brethren, knowing that as such we will incur a [1]stricter judgment. **2** For we all *a*stumble in many *ways.* *b*If anyone does not stumble in [1]what he says, he is a *c*perfect man, able to *d*bridle the whole body as well. **3** Now *a*if we put the bits into the horses' mouths so that they will obey us, we direct their entire body as well. **4** Look at the ships also, though they are so great and are driven by strong winds, are still directed by a very small rudder wherever the inclination of the pilot desires. **5** So also the tongue is a small part of the body, and *yet* it *a*boasts of great things. *b*See how great a forest is set aflame by such a small fire! **6** And *a*the tongue is a fire, the *very* world of iniquity; the tongue is set among our members as that which *b*defiles the entire body, and sets on fire the course of *our* [1]life, and is set on fire by [2]hell. **7** For every [1]species of beasts and birds, of reptiles and creatures of the sea, is tamed and has been tamed by the human [1]race. **8** But no one can tame the tongue; *it is* a restless evil *and* full of *a*deadly poison. **9** With it we bless *a*our Lord and Father, and with it we curse men, *b*who have been made in the likeness of God; **10** from the same mouth come *both* blessing and cursing. My brethren, these things ought not to be this way. **11** Does a fountain send out from the same opening *both* [1]fresh and bitter *water?* **12** *a*Can a fig tree, my brethren, produce olives, or a vine produce figs? Nor *can* salt water produce [1]fresh.

[Wisdom] 13 Who among you is wise and understanding? *a*Let him show by his *b*good behavior his deeds in the gentleness of wisdom. **14** But if you have bitter *a*jealousy and [1]selfish ambition in your heart, do not be arrogant and *so* lie against *b*the truth. **15** This wisdom is not that which comes down *a*from above, but is *b*earthly, [1]*c*natural, *d*demonic. **16** For where *a*jealousy and [1]selfish ambition exist, [2]there is disorder and every evil thing. **17** But the wisdom *a*from above is first *b*pure, then *c*peaceable, *d*gentle, [1]reasonable, *e*full of mercy and good fruits, *f*unwavering, without *g*hypocrisy. **18** And the [1]*a*seed whose fruit is righteousness is sown in peace [2]by those who make peace.

Discussion

Questioning the Passage

1. Is the judgment from God or other people? (v. 1)

    The author is referring to the final judgment which occurs before God at the end of one's life. It should be noted that teachers are often judged by their students and today schoolteachers sometimes have to absorb the grief from parents who believe their children before the teacher.

2. What does verse one through five mean?

    The author warns against too many people aspiring to be teachers because they will face a stricter judgment. Teaching carries great responsibility, and those who teach are held to a higher standard. James acknowledges everyone makes mistakes, especially in their speech. However, if someone can control their tongue, they show maturity and self-discipline. James uses the analogy of a horse's bit. Just as a small bit controls a powerful horse, our words have a significant impact on our lives. Similarly, a ship's small rudder determines its course, even in adverse conditions. Our tongues may seem insignificant, but they steer our lives. The author emphasizes the power of the tongue. Although small, it can ignite destructive fires—both literally and metaphorically. The author encourages us to control our speech because it shapes our lives. Taming our tongues leads to maturity and self-discipline, impacting our actions and relationships.

3. What does verse 5b through 12 mean?

    This is a group of metaphors that the author uses to exemplify his point. Words can be used to hurt people as much as physical weapons.

4. Why is there a difference in verse six between the Peshitta and NASB in the final phrase "by hell?"

The "by hell" has been added to several English verses. The original Greek version does not have "by hell." The idea of fire in hell was developed during the Medieval period. Since the book of James was written in 40 CE and the Middle Ages was 1100 to 1500 CE the author would not have added it.

5. What do verses fourteen and sixteen mean?

In James 3:14-16, the author provides a powerful warning about the dangers of bitter envy and selfish ambition. The author warns us about the dangers of allowing these negative traits to establish themselves in our hearts. If we harbor bitterness and selfishness, we should not boast or deceive ourselves. The passage emphasizes the importance of authenticity and truthfulness. The author contrasts this false wisdom with true heavenly wisdom. The worldly wisdom driven by envy and ambition is not aligned with God's principles. It is characterized by earthly desires, lack of spiritual insight, and even demonic influence. The author drives home the consequences of harboring envy and selfish ambition. They lead to chaos, disorder, and harmful actions. When our hearts are consumed by these negative traits, our lives become a breeding ground for destructive behavior. The author encourages us to seek heavenly wisdom, avoid envy and selfishness, and pursue truth and authenticity. Let us strive for a heart that reflects God's love and grace, rather than one tainted by jealousy and self-centeredness.

Thoughts

Being a teacher of the Word of the LORD is a difficult task and must be taken seriously. Incorrect teaching will become critical not only during one's life but in the LORD's decision on judgment day. Be careful what you teach.

Language

Peshitta	New American Standard 1995
James 4:1 Whence is it, that there are among you fightings and broils? Is it not from the lusts, which war in your members? **2** Ye covet, and possess not; and ye kill, and envy, and effect nothing: and ye fight and make attacks; and ye have not, because ye ask not. **3** Ye ask, and receive not; because ye ask wickedly, that ye may pamper your lusts. **4** Ye adulterers, know ye not, that the love of the world is hostility towards God? He therefore who chooseth to be a lover of this world, is the enemy of God. **5** Or think ye, that the scripture hath vainly said: The spirit dwelling in us lusteth with envy? **6** But our Lord hath given us more grace. Therefore he said: The Lord humbleth the lofty, and giveth grace to the lowly. **7** Subject yourselves therefore to God; and stand firm against Satan, and he will flee from you. **8** Draw nigh to God, and he will draw nigh to you. Cleanse your hands, ye sinners: sanctify your hearts, ye divided in mind. **9** Humble yourselves, and mourn: let your laughter be turned into mourning, and your joy into grief. **10** Humble yourselves before the Lord, and he will exalt you. **11** Speak not against each other, my brethren; for he that speaketh against his brother, or judgeth his brother, speaketh against the law, and judgeth the law. And if thou judgest the law, thou art not a doer of the law, but its judge. **12**	**James 4:1** [1]What is the source of quarrels and [a]conflicts among you? [2]Is not the source your pleasures that wage [b]war in your members? **2** You lust and do not have; *so* you [a]commit murder. You are envious and cannot obtain; *so* you fight and quarrel. You do not have because you do not ask. **3** You ask and [a]do not receive, because you ask [1]with wrong motives, so that you may spend *it* [2]on your pleasures. **4** You [a]adulteresses, do you not know that friendship with [b]the world is [c]hostility toward God? [d]Therefore whoever wishes to be a friend of the world makes himself an enemy of God. **5** Or do you think that the Scripture [a]speaks to no purpose: "[1]He [2]jealously desires [b]the Spirit which He has made to dwell in us"? **6** But [a]He gives a greater grace. Therefore *it* says, "[cb]GOD IS OPPOSED TO THE PROUD, BUT GIVES GRACE TO THE HUMBLE." **7** [a]Submit therefore to God. [b]Resist the devil and he will flee from you. **8** [a]Draw near to God and He will draw near to you. [b]Cleanse your hands, you sinners; and [c]purify your hearts, you [d]double-minded. **9** [a]Be miserable and mourn and weep; let your laughter be turned into mourning and your joy to gloom. **10** [a]Humble yourselves in the presence of the Lord, and He will exalt you.

There is one Law-giver and Judge, who can make alive, and [can] destroy: but who art thou, that thou judgest thy neighbor? **13** But what shall we say of those, who say: To-day or to-morrow we will go to such or such a city, and will abide there a year; and we will traffic, and get gain? **14** And they know not what will be to-morrow: for what is our life, but an exhalation that is seen a little while, and then vanisheth and is gone? **15** Whereas they should say: If the Lord please, and we live, we will do this or that. **16** They glory in their vaunting. All such glorying is evil. **17** He that knoweth the good, and doeth it not, to him is sin.

James 4:11 *a*Do not speak against one another, *b*brethren. He who speaks against a brother or *c*judges his brother, speaks against *d*the law and judges the law; but if you judge the law, you are not *e*a doer of the law but a judge *of it.* **12** There is *only* one *a*Lawgiver and Judge, the One who is *b*able to save and to destroy; but *c*who are you who judge your neighbor?

James 4:13 *a*Come now, you who say, *"b*Today or tomorrow we will go to such and such a city, and spend a year there and engage in business and make a profit." **14** *1*Yet you do not know *2*what your life will be like tomorrow. *a*You are *just* a vapor that appears for a little while and then vanishes away. **15** *1*Instead, *you ought* to say, *"a*If the Lord wills, we will live and also do this or that." **16** But as it is, you boast in your *1*arrogance; *a*all such boasting is evil. **17** Therefore, *a*to one who knows *the 1*right thing to do and does not do it, to him it is sin.

James 4:1
[1]Lit *From where wars and from where fightings*
[2]Lit Are they *not from here,* from your
[a]Titus 3:9
[b]Rom 7:23

James 4:2
[a]James 5:6; 1 John 3:15

James 4:3
[1]Lit *wickedly*
[2]Lit *in*
[a]1 John 3:22; 5:14

James 4:4
[a]Jer 2:2; Ezek 16:32
[b]James 1:27
[c]Rom 8:7; 1 John 2:15
[d]Matt 6:24; John 15:19

James 4:5
[1]Or *The spirit which He has made to dwell in us lusts with envy*
[2]Lit *desires to jealousy*
[a]Num 23:19
[b]1 Cor 6:19; 2 Cor 6:16

James 4:6
[a]Is 54:7f; Matt 13:12
[b]Ps 138:6; Prov 3:34; Matt 23:12; 1 Pet 5:5

James 4:7
[a]1 Pet 5:6
[b]Eph 4:27; 6:11f; 1 Pet 5:8f

James 4:8
[a]2 Chr 15:2; Zech 1:3; Mal 3:7; Heb 7:19
[b]Job 17:9; Is 1:16; 1 Tim 2:8

ᶜJer 4:14; James 3:17; 1 Pet 1:22; 1 John 3:3
ᵈJames 1:8

James 4:9
ᵃNeh 8:9; Prov 14:13; Luke 6:25

James 4:10
ᵃJob 5:11; Ezek 21:26; Luke 1:52; James 4:6

James 4:11
ᵃ2 Cor 12:20; James 5:9; 1 Pet 2:1
ᵇJames 1:16; 5:7, 9, 10
ᶜMatt 7:1; Rom 14:4
ᵈJames 2:8
ᵉJames 1:22

James 4:12
ᵃIs 33:22; James 5:9
ᵇMatt 10:28
ᶜRom 14:4

James 4:13
ᵃJames 5:1
ᵇProv 27:1; Luke 12:18-20

James 4:14
[1]Lit *Who do not*
[2]Or *what* will happen *tomorrow. What kind of life is yours?*
ᵃJob 7:7; Ps 39:5; 102:3; 144:4

James 4:15
[1]Lit *Instead of your saying*
ᵃActs 18:21

James 4:16
[1]Or *pretensions*
ᵃ1 Cor 5:6

James 4:17
[1]Or *good*
ᵃLuke 12:47; John 9:41; 2 Pet 2:21

ames 4:1   Πόθεν πόλεμοι καὶ μάχαι ἐν ὑμῖν; Οὐκ ἐντεῦθεν ἐκ τῶν ἡδονῶν ὑμῶν τῶν στρατευομένων ἐν τοῖς μέλεσιν ὑμῶν; **2** Ἐπιθυμεῖτε, καὶ οὐκ ἔχετε· φονεύετε καὶ ζηλοῦτε, καὶ οὐ δύνασθε ἐπιτυχεῖν· μάχεσθε καὶ πολεμεῖτε, οὐκ ἔχετε διὰ τὸ μὴ αἰτεῖσθαι ὑμᾶς· **3** αἰτεῖτε, καὶ οὐ λαμβάνετε, διότι κακῶς αἰτεῖσθε, ἵνα ἐν ταῖς ἡδοναῖς ὑμῶν δαπανήσητε. **4** Μοιχοὶ καὶ μοιχαλίδες, οὐκ οἴδατε ὅτι ἡ φιλία τοῦ κόσμου ἔχθρα τοῦ θεοῦ ἐστιν; Ὃς ἂν οὖν βουληθῇ φίλος εἶναι τοῦ κόσμου, ἐχθρὸς τοῦ θεοῦ καθίσταται. **5** Ἢ δοκεῖτε ὅτι κενῶς ἡ γραφὴ λέγει, Πρὸς φθόνον ἐπιποθεῖ τὸ πνεῦμα ὃ κατῴκησεν ἐν ἡμῖν; **6** Μείζονα δὲ δίδωσιν χάριν· διὸ λέγει, Ὁ θεὸς ὑπερηφάνοις ἀντιτάσσεται, ταπεινοῖς δὲ δίδωσιν χάριν. **7** Ὑποτάγητε οὖν τῷ θεῷ· ἀντίστητε ⸀δὲ⸀ τῷ διαβόλῳ, καὶ φεύξεται ἀφ᾽ ὑμῶν. **8** Ἐγγίσατε τῷ θεῷ, καὶ ἐγγιεῖ ὑμῖν· καθαρίσατε χεῖρας, ἁμαρτωλοί, καὶ ἁγνίσατε καρδίας, δίψυχοι. **9** Ταλαιπωρήσατε καὶ πενθήσατε καὶ κλαύσατε· ὁ γέλως ὑμῶν εἰς πένθος μεταστραφήτω, καὶ ἡ χαρὰ εἰς κατήφειαν. **10** Ταπεινώθητε ἐνώπιον τοῦ κυρίου, καὶ ὑψώσει ὑμᾶς.

James 4:11   Μὴ καταλαλεῖτε ἀλλήλων, ἀδελφοί. Ὁ καταλαλῶν ἀδελφοῦ, καὶ κρίνων τὸν ἀδελφὸν αὐτοῦ, καταλαλεῖ νόμου, καὶ κρίνει νόμον· εἰ δὲ νόμον κρίνεις, οὐκ εἶ ποιητὴς νόμου, ἀλλὰ κριτής. **12** Εἷς ἐστιν ὁ νομοθέτης, ὁ δυνάμενος σῶσαι καὶ ἀπολέσαι· σὺ δὲ τίς εἶ ὃς κρίνεις τὸν ἕτερον;

James 4:13   Ἄγε νῦν οἱ λέγοντες, Σήμερον καὶ αὔριον πορευσώμεθα εἰς τήνδε τὴν πόλιν, καὶ ποιήσωμεν ἐκεῖ ἐνιαυτὸν ἕνα, καὶ ἐμπορευσώμεθα, καὶ κερδήσωμεν· **14** οἵτινες οὐκ ἐπίστασθε τὸ τῆς αὔριον. Ποία γὰρ ἡ ζωὴ ὑμῶν; Ἀτμὶς γὰρ ⸀ἔσται⸀ ἡ πρὸς ὀλίγον φαινομένη, ἔπειτα δὲ καὶ ἀφανιζομένη. **15** Ἀντὶ τοῦ λέγειν ὑμᾶς, Ἐὰν ὁ κύριος θελήσῃ, καὶ ζήσωμεν, καὶ ποιήσωμεν τοῦτο ἢ ἐκεῖνο. **16** Νῦν δὲ καυχᾶσθε ἐν ταῖς ἀλαζονείαις ὑμῶν· πᾶσα καύχησις τοιαύτη πονηρά ἐστιν. **17** Εἰδότι οὖν καλὸν ποιεῖν καὶ μὴ ποιοῦντι, ἁμαρτία αὐτῷ ἐστιν.

Language

Process of Discovery

Linguistics Section

Linguistic Structure

A 1 [1]What is the source of quarrels and [a]conflicts among you? [2]Is not the source your pleasures that wage [b]war in your members? **2** You lust and do not have; *so* you [a]commit murder. You are envious and cannot obtain; *so* you fight and quarrel. You do not have because you do not ask. **3** You ask and [a]do not receive, because you ask [1]with wrong motives, so that you may spend *it* [2]on your pleasures.

B 4 You [a]adulteresses, do you not know that friendship with [b]the world is [c]hostility toward God? [d]Therefore whoever wishes to be a friend of the world makes himself an enemy of God. **5** Or do you think that the Scripture [a]speaks to no purpose: "'[1]He [2]jealously desires [b]the Spirit which He has made to dwell in us"? **6** But [a]He gives a greater grace. Therefore *it* says, "[b]GOD IS OPPOSED TO THE PROUD, BUT GIVES GRACE TO THE HUMBLE."

B' 7 [a]Submit therefore to God. [b]Resist the devil and he will flee from you. **8** [a]Draw near to God and He will draw near to you. [b]Cleanse your hands, you sinners; and [c]purify your hearts, you [d]double-minded. **9** [a]Be miserable and mourn and weep; let your laughter be turned into mourning and your joy to gloom. **10** [a]Humble yourselves in the presence of the Lord, and He will exalt you.

A' 11 [a]Do not speak against one another, [b]brethren. He who speaks against a brother or [c]judges his brother, speaks against [d]the law and judges the law; but if you judge the law, you are not [e]a doer of the law but a judge *of it*. **12** There is *only* one [a]Lawgiver and Judge, the One who is [b]able to save and to destroy; but [c]who are you who judge your neighbor?

[Fate] 13 [a]Come now, you who say, "[b]Today or tomorrow we will go to such and such a city, and spend a year there and engage in business and make a profit." **14** [1]Yet you do not know [2]what your life will be like tomorrow. [a]You are *just* a vapor that appears for a little while and then vanishes away.

[Avoid sin] 15 [1]Instead, *you ought* to say, "*If the Lord wills, we will live and also do this or that.*" **16** But as it is, you boast in your [1]arrogance; [a]all such boasting is evil. **17** Therefore, [a]to one who knows *the* [1]right thing to do and does not do it, to him it is sin.

Discussion

This chapter comprises one simple chiasm. The chapter concentrates on the strength of Satan and how, when one's sins, one can give oneself to Satan.

Questioning the Passage

1. What does "war in your members" mean? (v. 1)

   Essentially, the author highlights the internal struggle within individuals—the passions and desires that can lead to strife and discord. So, the phrase "wage war in your body's parts" refers to the inner battle between conflicting desires and emotions. It is a reminder to seek peace and address conflicts constructively rather than allowing them to escalate.[17]

2. What are the wrong motives in prayer? (v. 3)

   The prayers of many of the people in the community that the author was writing to were not being answered. Prayers that sought material things justify their wants, desires, and passions and not because there was a real need.

3. What does verse four mean?

   The word "adulterers" is used figuratively. It refers to those who have departed from truth in spiritual matters for the gain of material things of this world.

---

[17] 1. "James 4:1," BibleRef.com, accessed May 27, 2024, https://www.bibleref.com/James/4/James-4-1.html.

Yeshua called them the false religious people and used the word adulterers to refer to them. They were more concerned about material gains in this world rather than spiritual matters. The author is not condemning wealth rather he indicates an inordinate desire for material possessions.[18]

4. What is the purpose of the Scripture? (v. 5)

Some people in the community must have thought that the Scripture has no purpose in life. They believed it was a meaningless document. The author is saying that the Scriptures are very important for learning, edification, comfort, doctrine, reproof, correction, or instructions in righteousness. The Scriptures are not an empty document but carry weight and significance. The Scripture is a guide that takes us toward a faithful relationship with God.

5. What does "draw near to God" mean? (v. 8)

To "draw near" means to approach God intentionally, seeking a closer relationship with Him. It involves moving from a distance to a position of intimacy and communion. The author invites us to come into God's presence, not as distant observers but as active participants.

The author gives us a formula for drawing close to God. First, we need to confess our sins—acknowledge our wrongdoings and turn away from them. One must recognize that Jesus has already paid the price for our sins, allowing us to receive God's forgiveness and remember those sins no more.

---

[18] 1. Rocco A. Errico and George M. Lamsa, *Aramaic Light on James through Revelation: A Commentary Based on Aramaic, the Language of Jesus, and Ancient near Eastern Customs* (Smyrna, GA: Noohra Foundation, 2006).

The author emphasizes the need to "cleanse your hands." This metaphorical language suggests that we should purify our actions and behavior. It is a call to live righteously and avoid sinful practices.

Beyond external actions, the author also urges us to "purify your hearts." This involves inner transformation—aligning our desires, thoughts, and motives with God's will. It is about wholehearted devotion and loyalty to God.

The author refers to those who are "double-minded." This means wavering between two allegiances—God and the world. To draw near to God, we must wholeheartedly choose Him over any divided loyalties.

The author assures us that when we draw near to God, He reciprocates. God responds by drawing near to us. It is a beautiful exchange—a divine invitation met with divine presence.

In summary, "drawing near to God" involves confession, cleansing, inner purity, and unwavering devotion. It is an invitation to experience God's closeness and intimacy.[19]

6. What does "cleansing your hands" mean? (v. 8)

This phrase means removing all the evil from one's thoughts and spirit.

---

[19] 1. Karen O'Reilly, "Devotional Bible Study: Draw Closer to God: James 4:8.," scriptural, June 10, 2021, https://www.scripturalgrace.com/post/devotional-bible-study-draw-closer-to-god-james-4-8.

7. What does verse nine mean?

The author calls readers who may have compromised with worldly desires to get right with God. The verse emphasizes a shift from pursuing personal desires (which often leads to laughter and joy) to a posture of sorrow and repentance.

It is not about constant misery but recognizing the need for change and turning away from sinful paths.

The author encourages believers to feel the weight of their actions—to recognize their spiritual poverty and need for God. This involves genuine sorrow over sin. It is not mere gloom or melancholy, but heartfelt remorse.

Tears symbolize repentance and a desire for transformation.

The author affirms that true conversion involves both inward contrition (a change of heart) and outward lamentation (expressing sorrow).

The process of repentance leads to a deeper relationship with God and a turning away from worldly pursuits.

The author urges us to embrace godly sorrow, recognize our need for forgiveness, and allow our laughter to be transformed into genuine mourning—a step toward reconciliation with God.

8. What does it mean to be exalted by the Lord? (v. 10)

To exalt the Lord, we must first humble ourselves in the presence of God. This involves recognizing our own limitations, weaknesses, and need for God. It is an attitude of submission, acknowledging that God is greater than us and deserving of honor and praise.

Our humility is not just a public show. It is about our heart posture before God. We humble ourselves before His presence, recognizing His sovereignty and majesty.

9. How does the author justify his words against the people in verse eleven and twelve?

The author begins by urging believers not to slander or speak evil against each other. When we criticize or judge fellow believers, we are essentially speaking against God's law because that law commands us to love one another and treat each other with kindness and respect.

The author shows that when we judge others, we position ourselves as judges over the law. However, our role is not to judge the law but to obey it. By judging others, we undermine our obedience to God's commands.

The author emphasizes only God has the authority to establish laws and pass judgment. He is both the lawgiver (the one who sets the standards) and the judge (the one who evaluates our actions). Our responsibility is to submit to God's authority rather than assuming His role.

In summary, James reminds us to treat one another with love, avoid slander, and recognize that God alone holds the ultimate authority to judge. We need to focus on obedience and leave judgment to Him.[20]

---

[20] 1. BibleStudyTools Staff, "James 4:11-12 - Brothers and Sisters, Do Not Slander One Another. ...," Bible Study Tools, accessed May 27, 2024, https://www.biblestudytools.com/james/passage/?q=james%2B4%3A11-12.

10. What does verse thirteen to seventeen mean?

The author begins by addressing those who boast about their future. "Today or tomorrow, we shall go to such-and-such a city, spend a year there, engage in business, and make a profit." The problem lies not in planning itself, but in secular planning that excludes God. It assumes control over the future without acknowledging His sovereignty. James does not condemn planning; rather, he highlights the need for God-centered planning.

The author reminds us of our mortality: "You are just a vapor that appears for a little while and then vanishes away." Our lives are fleeting, like morning mist. We cannot predict tomorrow with certainty. Instead of presuming control, we should humbly say, "If the Lord wills, we shall live and also do this or that."

The author rebukes boasting rooted in arrogance: "But as it is, you boast in your arrogance; all such boasting is evil." Arrogance blinds us from acknowledging our dependence on God and leads to flawed planning. True wisdom acknowledges our limitations and seeks alignment with God's will.

The author concludes: "Therefore, to one who knows the right thing to do, and does not do it, to him it is sin." Obedience to God's will is crucial. Ignoring it leads to sin. Our plans should align with His purposes, seeking His guidance and surrendering our pride.

The author encourages us to recognize our frailty, submit to God's will, and humbly plan with His guidance.[21]

---

[21] 1. April 8 and Matt McCraw, "An Arrogant Vapor (James 4:13-17)," First Baptist Church, April 8, 2018, https://fbcbartow.org/sermons/arrogant-vapor-james-413-17/.

Verse Comparison of citations or proof text

1. **6** But *ª*He gives a greater grace. Therefore *it* says, ""*ᵇ*GOD IS OPPOSED TO THE PROUD, BUT GIVES GRACE TO THE HUMBLE.""

    Psalm 138:6 High though the LORD is, He sees the lowly; lofty, He perceives from afar.

Thoughts

It is important that we try to avoid sin at all costs. When one starts to sin and Satan can invade one's soul easily. Fights between people, especially believers in Yeshua, should never occur. Obviously, disagreements will occur from time to time, but it is important to resolve them as quickly as possible so that harmony is always maintained.

Chapter Five

Language

Peshitta	New American Standard 1995
James 5:1 O ye rich ones, wail and weep, on account of the miseries that are coming upon you. **2** For your wealth is spoiled and putrid; and your garments are moth-eaten: **3** and your gold and your silver have contracted rust; and the rust of them will be testimony against you; and it will eat your flesh. Ye have heaped up a fire to you against the latter days. **4** Behold, the wages of the laborers who have reaped your ground, which ye have wrongfully retained, crieth out; and the clamor of the reapers hath entered the ears of the Lord of Sabaoth. **5** For ye have lived in pleasure on the earth, and revelled, and feasted your bodies as in a day of slaughter. **6** Ye have condemned and slain the just, and none resisted you. **7** But, my brethren, be ye patient until the advent of the Lord; like the husbandman, who waiteth for the precious fruits of his ground, and is patient as to them, until he receive the early and the latter rain. **8** So also be ye patient, and fortify your hearts; for the advent of our Lord draweth nigh **9** Be not querulous one against another, my brethren, lest ye be judged: for lo, the judgment standeth before the door. **10** For patience in your afflictions, my brethren, take to you the example of the prophets, who spoke in the name of the Lord. **11** For lo, we ascribe blessedness to them who have borne suffering. Ye have heard of the patience of Job; and ye have seen the result which the	**James 5:1** [a]Come now, [b]you rich, [c]weep and howl for your miseries which are coming upon you. **2** [a]Your riches have rotted and your garments have become moth-eaten. **3** Your gold and your silver have rusted; and their rust will be a witness against you and will consume your flesh like fire. It is [a]in the last days that you have stored up your treasure! **4** Behold, [a]the pay of the laborers who mowed your fields, *and* which has been withheld by you, cries out *against you;* and [b]the outcry of those who did the harvesting has reached the ears of [c]the Lord of [1]Sabaoth. **5** You have [a]lived luxuriously on the earth and led a life of wanton pleasure; you have [1]fattened your hearts in [b]a day of slaughter. **6** You have condemned and [1a]put to death [b]the righteous *man;* he does not resist you. **James 5:7** Therefore be patient, [a]brethren, [b]until the coming of the Lord. [c]The farmer waits for the precious produce of the soil, being patient about it, until [1]it gets [d]the early and late rains. **8** [a]You too be patient; [b]strengthen your hearts, for [c]the coming of the Lord is [d]near. **9** [a]Do not [1]complain, [b]brethren, against one another, so that you yourselves may not be judged; behold, [c]the Judge is standing [2d]right at the [3]door. **10** As an example, [a]brethren, of suffering and patience, take [b]the prophets who spoke in the name of the Lord. **11** We count those [a]blessed who endured. You

Lord wrought for him: for the Lord is merciful and compassionate. **12** But above all things, my brethren, swear ye not; neither by heaven, nor by the earth, nor by any other oath: but let your language be yes, yes, and no, no, lest ye become obnoxious to judgment. **13** And if any of you shall be in affliction, let him pray; or if he be joyous, let him sing psalms. **14** And if one is sick, let him call for the elders of the church; and let them pray for him, and anoint him with oil in the name of our Lord: **15** and the prayer of faith will heal him who is sick, and our Lord will raise him up; and if sins have been committed by him, they will be forgiven him. **16** And confess ye your faults one to another, and pray ye one for another, that ye may be healed; for great is the efficacy of the prayer which a righteous man prayeth. **17** Elijah also was a man of sensations like us, and he prayed that rain might not descend upon the earth; and it descended not, for three years and six months. **18** And again he prayed, and the heavens gave rain, and the earth gave forth its fruits. **19** My brethren, if one of you err from the way of truth, and any one convert him from his error; **20** let him know, that he who turneth the sinner from the error of his way, will resuscitate his soul from death, and will cover the multitude of his sins.

have heard of [b]the [1]endurance of Job and have seen [c]the [2]outcome of the Lord's dealings, that [d]the Lord is full of compassion and *is* merciful.

James 5:12 But above all, [a]my brethren, [b]do not swear, either by heaven or by earth or with any other oath; but [1]your yes is to be yes, and your no, no, so that you may not fall under judgment.

James 5:13 Is anyone among you [a]suffering? [b]*Then* he must pray. Is anyone cheerful? He is to [c]sing praises. **14** Is anyone among you sick? *Then* he must call for [a]the elders of the church and they are to pray over him, [1b]anointing him with oil in the name of the Lord; **15** and the [a]prayer [1]offered in faith will [2b]restore the one who is sick, and the Lord will [c]raise him up, and if he has committed sins, [3]they will be forgiven him. **16** Therefore, [a]confess your sins to one another, and pray for one another so that you may be [b]healed. [c]The effective [1]prayer of a righteous man can accomplish much. **17** Elijah was [a]a man with a nature like ours, and [b]he prayed [1]earnestly that it would not rain, and it did not rain on the earth for [c]three years and six months. **18** Then he [a]prayed again, and [b]the [1]sky [2]poured rain and the earth produced its fruit.

James 5:19 My brethren, [a]if any among you strays from [b]the truth and one turns him back, **20** let him know that [1]he who turns a sinner from the error of his way will [a]save his soul from death and will [b]cover a multitude of sins.

James 5:1
[a]James 4:13
[b]Luke 6:24; 1 Tim 6:9
[c]Is 13:6; 15:3; Ezek 30:2

James 5:2
[a]Job 13:28; Is 50:9; Matt 6:19f

James 5:3
[a]James 5:7, 8

James 5:4
[1]I.e. Hosts
[a]Lev 19:13; Job 24:10f; Jer 22:13; Mal 3:5
[b]Ex 2:23; Deut 24:15; Job 31:38f
[c]Rom 9:29; Is 5:9

James 5:5
[1]Lit *nourished*
[a]Ezek 16:49; Luke 16:19; 1 Tim 5:6; 2 Pet 2:13
[b]Jer 12:3; 25:34

James 5:6
[1]Or *murdered*
[a]James 4:2
[b]Heb 10:38; 1 Pet 4:18

James 5:7
[1]Or *he*
[a]James 4:11; 5:9, 10
[b]John 21:22; 1 Thess 2:19
[c]Gal 6:9
[d]Deut 11:14; Jer 5:24; Joel 2:23

James 5:8
[a]Luke 21:19

[b]1 Thess 3:13
[c]John 21:22; 1 Thess 2:19
[d]Rom 13:11, 12; 1 Pet 4:7

James 5:9
[1]Lit *groan*
[2]Lit *before*
[3]Lit *doors*
[a]James 4:11
[b]James 5:7, 10
[c]1 Cor 4:5; James 4:12; 1 Pet 4:5
[d]Matt 24:33; Mark 13:29

James 5:10
[a]James 4:11; 5:7, 9
[b]Matt 5:12

James 5:11
[1]Or *steadfastness*
[2]Lit *end of the Lord*
[a]Matt 5:10; 1 Pet 3:14
[b]Job 1:21f; 2:10
[c]Job 42:10, 12
[d]Ex 34:6; Ps 103:8

James 5:12
[1]Lit *yours is to be yes, yes, and no, no*
[a]James 1:16
[b]Matt 5:34-37

James 5:13
[a]James 5:10
[b]Ps 50:15
[c]1 Cor 14:15; Col 3:16

James 5:14
[1]Lit *having anointed*
[a]Acts 11:30
[b]Mark 6:13; 16:18

James 5:15

¹Lit *of*
²Or *save*
³Lit *it*
ᵃJames 1:6
ᵇ1 Cor 1:21; James 5:20
ᶜJohn 6:39; 2 Cor 4:14

James 5:16
¹Lit *supplication*
ᵃMatt 3:6; Mark 1:5; Acts 19:18
ᵇHeb 12:13; 1 Pet 2:24
ᶜGen 18:23-32; John 9:31

James 5:17
¹Lit *with prayer*
ᵃActs 14:15
ᵇ1 Kin 17:1; 18:1
ᶜLuke 4:25

James 5:18
¹Lit *heaven*
²Lit *gave*
ᵃ1 Kin 18:42
ᵇ1 Kin 18:45

James 5:19
ᵃMatt 18:15; Gal 6:1
ᵇJames 3:14

James 5:20
¹Lit *he who has turned*
ᵃRom 11:14; 1 Cor 1:21; James 1:21
ᵇProv 10:12; 1 Pet 4:8

Koine Greek

James 5:1   Αγε νυν οι πλουσιοι, κλαυσατε ολολυζοντες επι ταις ταλαιπωριαις υμων ταις επερχομεναις. [2] ο πλουτος υμων σεσηπεν και τα ιματια υμων σητοβρωτα γεγονεν, [3] ο χρυσος υμων και ο αργυρος κατιωται και ο ιος αυτων εις μαρτυριον υμιν εσται και φαγεται τας σαρκας υμων ως πυρ. εθησαυρισατε εν εσχαταις ημεραις. [4] ιδου ο μισθος των εργατων των αμησαντων τας χωρας υμων ο απεστερημενος αφ' υμων κραζει, και αι βοαι των θερισαντων *εις τα ωτα κυριου σαβαωθ* εισεληλυθασιν. [5] ετρυφησατε επι της γης και εσπαταλησατε, εθρεψατε τας καρδιας υμων *εν ημερα σφαγης,* [6] κατεδικασατε, εφονευσατε τον δικαιον· ουκ αντιτασσεται υμιν.

James 5:7   Μακροθυμησατε ουν, αδελφοι, εως της παρουσιας του κυριου. ιδου ο γεωργος εκδεχεται τον τιμιον καρπον της γης μακροθυμων επ' αυτω, εως λαβη προιμον και οψιμον. [8] μακροθυμησατε και υμεις, στηριξατε τας καρδιας υμων, οτι η παρουσια του κυριου ηγγικεν. [9] μη στεναζετε, αδελφοι, κατ' αλληλων, ινα μη κριθητε· ιδου ο κριτης προ των θυρων εστηκεν. [10] υποδειγμα λαβετε, αδελφοι, της κακοπαθειας και της μακροθυμιας τους προφητας οι ελαλησαν εν τω ονοματι κυριου. [11] ιδου μακαριζομεν τους υπομειναντας· την υπομονην Ιωβ ηκουσατε και το τελος κυριου ειδετε, οτι πολυσπλαγχνος εστιν ο κυριος και οικτιρμων.

James 5:12   Προ παντων δε, αδελφοι μου, μη ομνυετε μητε τον ουρανον μητε την γην μητε αλλον τινα ορκον· ητω δε υμων το ναι ναι και το ου ου, ινα μη υπο κρισιν πεσητε.

James 5:13   Κακοπαθει τις εν υμιν, προσευχεσθω· ευθυμει τις, ψαλλετω· [14] ασθενει τις εν υμιν, προσκαλεσασθω τους πρεσβυτερους της εκκλησιας και προσευξασθωσαν επ' αυτον αλειψαντες αυτον ελαιω εν τω ονοματι του κυριου. [15] και η ευχη της πιστεως σωσει τον καμνοντα και εγερει αυτον ο κυριος· καν αμαρτιας η πεποιηκως, αφεθησεται αυτω. [16] εξομολογεισθε ουν αλληλοις τας αμαρτιας και ευχεσθε υπερ αλληλων, οπως ιαθητε. πολυ ισχυει δεησις δικαιου ενεργουμενη. [17] Ηλιας ανθρωπος ην ομοιοπαθης ημιν και προσευχη προσηυξατο του μη βρεξαι, και ουκ εβρεξεν επι της γης ενιαυτους τρεις και μηνας εξ· [18] και παλιν προσηυξατο, και ο ουρανος υετον εδωκεν και η γη εβλαστησεν τον καρπον αυτης.

James 5:19   Αδελφοι μου, εαν τις εν υμιν πλανηθη απο της αληθειας και επιστρεψη τις αυτον, [20] γινωσκετω οτι ο επιστρεψας αμαρτωλον εκ πλανης οδου αυτου σωσει ψυχην αυτου εκ θανατου και καλυψει πληθος αμαρτιων.

Language

  Process of Discovery

    Linguistics Section

    Linguistic Structure

[Rich people] 1   ^aCome now, ^byou rich, ^cweep and howl for your miseries which are coming upon you. **2** ^aYour riches have rotted and your garments have become moth-eaten. **3** Your gold and your silver have rusted; and their rust will be a witness against you and will consume your flesh like fire. It is ^ain the last days that you have stored up your treasure! **4** Behold, ^athe pay of the laborers who mowed your fields, *and* which has been withheld by you, cries out *against you;* and ^bthe outcry of those who did the harvesting has reached the ears of ^cthe Lord of ¹Sabaoth. **5** You have ^alived luxuriously on the earth and led a life of wanton pleasure; you have ¹fattened your hearts in ^ba day of slaughter. **6** You have condemned and ^{1a}put to death ^bthe righteous *man;* he does not resist you.

[End Times] 7   Therefore be patient, ^abrethren, ^buntil the coming of the Lord. ^cThe farmer waits for the precious produce of the soil, being patient about it, until ¹it gets ^dthe early and late rains. **8** ^aYou too be patient; ^bstrengthen your hearts, for ^cthe coming of the Lord is ^dnear. **9** ^aDo not ¹complain, ^bbrethren, against one another, so that you yourselves may not be judged; behold, ^cthe Judge is standing ^{2d}right at the ³door. **10** As an example, ^abrethren, of suffering and patience, take ^bthe prophets who spoke in the name of the Lord. **11** We count those ^ablessed who endured. You have heard of ^bthe ¹endurance of Job and have seen ^cthe ²outcome of the Lord's dealings, that ^dthe Lord is full of compassion and *is* merciful.

[Oaths] 12   But above all, ^amy brethren, ^bdo not swear, either by heaven or by earth or with any other oath; but ¹your yes is to be yes, and your no, no, so that you may not fall under judgment.

[Suffering] 13   Is anyone among you ^asuffering? ^b*Then* he must pray. Is anyone cheerful? He is to ^csing praises. **14** Is anyone among you sick? *Then* he must call for ^athe elders of the church and they are to pray over him, ^{1b}anointing him with oil in the name of the Lord; **15** and the ^aprayer ¹offered in faith will ^{2b}restore the one who is sick, and the Lord will ^craise him up, and if he has committed sins, ³they will be forgiven him. **16** Therefore, ^aconfess your sins to one another, and pray for one another so that you may be ^bhealed. ^cThe effective ¹prayer of a righteous man can accomplish much. **17** Elijah was ^aa man with a nature like ours, and ^bhe prayed ¹earnestly that it would not rain, and it did not rain on the earth for ^cthree years and six months. **18** Then he ^aprayed again, and ^bthe ¹sky ²poured rain and the earth produced its fruit.

[**Conclusion**]19 My brethren, ^aif any among you strays from ^bthe truth and one turns him back, **20** let him know that ¹he who turns a sinner from the error of his way will ^asave his soul from death and will ^bcover a multitude of sins.

Discussion

The author hammers anyone who has any kind of wealth.

Questioning the Passage

1. What are the miseries because of the rich people? (v. 1)

   It has a powerful reminder about the impermanence of material wealth and the need for humility and compassion.

2. What do "your riches have rotted" and "garments have become moth-eaten" mean? (v. 2)

   The imagery of decaying wealth and moth-eaten clothing serves as a powerful reminder of the impermanence of material possessions and the need for humility and compassion.

3. What does "gold and silver have rusted" mean? (v. 3)

   The author continues his harsh condemnation of wealthy non-Christians who had been oppressing the poor. This includes abuse against the very Christians the author is writing to. He warns these rich oppressors that their wealth is as good as gone, including their gold and silver. The imagery of corroded wealth and the impending judgment serves as a powerful reminder of the impermanence of material possessions and the need for humility and compassion.

4. What was the "day of slaughter?" (v. 5)

The author continues his condemnation of wealthy landowners who oppressed the poor, including his Christian readers. The imagery emphasizes the impending judgment: just as food rots, garments become moth-eaten, and gold and silver corrode, their wealth will ultimately come to nothing. It serves as a powerful reminder that true riches come from a life lived in righteousness, patience, prayer, and care for others, rather than material wealth.

5. Who is the just (righteous man) in verse six?

The author offers his final charge against the wealthy oppressors he has been condemning for murder. Not only were they guilty of hoarding wealth while others suffered in poverty, cheating their workers out of earned wages, and living in self-indulgent luxury, but they had also literally caused the death of innocent or righteous individuals. The verse emphasizes that these victims did not resist their oppressors.

6. What does verse seven mean?

The author encourages suffering believers to be patient while awaiting the coming of the Lord. He draws an analogy with a farmer who patiently awaits the precious fruit of the earth, enduring both early and late rains. The message is clear. Just as the farmer expects the valuable harvest, believers should patiently await the fulfillment of God's promises, even in difficult times.

7. What happened to Job? (v. 11)

The Book of Job is an ancient biblical text that grapples with profound questions about suffering, divine justice, and human limitations.

- Job, a wealthy man from the land of Uz, is "blameless" and "upright."
- Satan challenges God, claiming that Job's goodness is only because of his blessings.
- God permits Satan to test Job's faith by inflicting immense suffering upon him.

2. Job's Trials:

- Job loses his livestock, servants, and ten children in a single day.
- Despite his grief, Job blesses God.
- Satan afflicts Job with painful sores, testing his resilience.

3. Conversations with Friends:

- Job's three friends—Eliphaz, Bildad, and Zophar—visit him.
- They engage in poetic dialogues, trying to make sense of Job's suffering.
- They suggest that Job's agony results from sin or wrongdoing.

4. Job's Lament and Questions:

- Job curses the day of his birth, longing for darkness.
- He questions God's justice and the purpose of human suffering.
- Job's friends offer various explanations, but Job remains steadfast.

5. God's Response:

- God appears in a whirlwind, challenging Job's understanding.
- God emphasizes His sovereignty and wisdom beyond human comprehension.
- Job humbly acknowledges God's authority and repents.

6. Restoration and Blessings:

- God rebukes Job's friends and restores his fortunes.

- o   Job receives twice as much wealth, along with new children.

The book invites us to wrestle with life's complexities, recognizing that God's ways often surpass our understanding.[22]

8. How does prayer resolve the items in verses 14 and 15?

The process of resolving troubles through prayer involves several key elements.

1. Calling for the Elders: If someone is ill, they should call for the elders of the church. These mature, faith-filled individuals play a crucial role.
2. Anointing with Oil: The elders pray over the ill person and anoint them with oil in the name of the Lord. This act symbolizes consecration, healing, and God's presence.
3. Prayer Offered in Faith: The critical factor is faith. When the elders pray in faith, believing in God's power and goodness, healing occurs. The Lord responds by restoring health.
4. Forgiveness of Sins: James also acknowledges that if the ill person has committed any sins, they will be forgiven.[23]

---

[22] 1. BibleProject, "Book of Job: Guide with Key Information and Resources," BibleProject, November 16, 2023, https://bibleproject.com/guides/book-of-job/.

[23] 1. collen ndhlovucollen ndhlovu   23.9k4646 gold badges192192 silver badges365365 bronze badges et al., "Prayer of Faith or Oil That Heals the Sick in James 5:14-15?," Biblical Hermeneutics Stack Exchange, October 1, 1965, https://hermeneutics.stackexchange.com/questions/45232/prayer-of-faith-or-oil-that-heals-the-sick-in-james-514-15.

9. What is the history of Elijah and the drought? (v. 17)

The story of Elijah and the Drought is found in the book of 1 Kings 17. Proclamation of drought by Elijah, a prophet, declared to King Ahab that there would be no dew or rain for the next two or three years. This drought was a consequence of Israel's disobedience and idolatry.

1. Brook Cherith:
   o God instructed Elijah to hide near Cherith Brook, east of the Jordan River.
   o Miraculously, ravens brought him food (bread and meat), and he drank water from the brook.
2. Widow in Zarephath:
   o When the brook dried up because of the prolonged drought, God directed Elijah to Zarephath.
   o There, a widow provided for him, even though she had only a handful of flour and oil left.
   o Elijah assured her that her supplies would not run out until rain returned.
3. Miraculous Provision:
   o As promised, the widow's flour and oil did not run out during the entire drought.
   o God sustained both Elijah and the widow.
4. Resurrection of the Widow's Son:
   o Tragedy struck when the widow's son fell ill and died.
   o Elijah prayed, and God restored the boy's life, demonstrating His power and compassion.

10. What do verses 19 and 20 say (whose sins are being covered)?

The author encourages believers to reach out to those who have strayed from the truth. He refers to individuals who were once part of the Christian community but have lost their way. The passage emphasizes the importance of helping one another return to the right path, just as someone might turn a wanderer back from their errant course. It's a call to support and restore fellow believers, recognizing that we have the power to choose, and that Christ's sacrifice has freed us from bondage.[24]

Culture Section

Questioning the passage

1. What does the statement of "yes, yes" and "no, no" mean?
   Saying this is equivalent to taking an oath. It means that what is being said is the truth.

Thoughts

Considering the economy of ancient Judea, it is understandable that the author has a hatred toward rich people. Interestingly, the ability for a rich person to repent is never explored. This book does not mention Yeshua at all. This was one reason why Martin Luther wanted to exclude the book from his German Bible.

---

[24] 1. Daniel Ploof, "James 5:19-20 - Message: Meaning: Reflection," Daniel Ploof, February 24, 2024, https://www.journeyintothewilderness.com/blog/2016/02/james-519-20-devotion.html.

Bibliography

8, April, and Matt McCraw. "An Arrogant Vapor (James 4:13-17)." First Baptist Church, April 8, 2018. https://fbcbartow.org/sermons/arrogant-vapor-james-413-17/.

BibleProject. "Book of Job: Guide with Key Information and Resources." BibleProject, November 16, 2023. https://bibleproject.com/guides/book-of-job/.

collen ndhlovucollen ndhlovu   23.9k4646 gold badges192192 silver badges365365 bronze badges, RuminatorRuminator   1, Sola GratiaSola Gratia   9, and FTLFTL   1133 bronze badges. "Prayer of Faith or Oil That Heals the Sick in James 5:14-15?" Biblical Hermeneutics Stack Exchange, October 1, 1965. https://hermeneutics.stackexchange.com/questions/45232/prayer-of-faith-or-oil-that-heals-the-sick-in-james-514-15.

Daniel Ploof. "James 5:19-20 - Message: Meaning: Reflection." Daniel Ploof, February 24, 2024. https://www.journeyintothewilderness.com/blog/2016/02/james-519-20-devotion.html.

Errico, Rocco A., and George M. Lamsa. *Aramaic light on james through revelation: A commentary based on Aramaic, the language of jesus, and ancient near eastern customs.* Smyma, GA: Noohra Foundation, 2006.

GotQuestions.org. "Home." GotQuestions.org, June 13, 2022. https://www.gotquestions.org/firstfruits-of-His-creatures.html.

GotQuestions.org. "Home." GotQuestions.org, March 16, 2022. https://www.gotquestions.org/blessed-is-the-man-who-perseveres-under-trial.html.

James 1:10 commentaries: And the rich man is to glory in his humiliation, because like flowering grass he will pass away. Accessed April 29, 2024. https://biblehub.com/commentaries/james/1-10.htm.

"James 1:10." BibleRef.com. Accessed April 29, 2024. https://www.bibleref.com/James/1/James-1-10.html.

"James 1:9." BibleRef.com. Accessed April 29, 2024. https://www.bibleref.com/James/1/James-1-9.html.

"James 2:10." BibleRef.com. Accessed May 11, 2024. https://www.bibleref.com/James/2/James-2-10.html.

"James 4:1." BibleRef.com. Accessed May 27, 2024. https://www.bibleref.com/James/4/James-4-1.html.

James Summary. Accessed April 29, 2024. https://biblehub.com/summary/james/1.htm.

O'Reilly, Karen. "Devotional Bible Study: Draw Closer to God: James 4:8." scriptural, June 10, 2021. https://www.scripturalgrace.com/post/devotional-bible-study-draw-closer-to-god-james-4-8.

Poor, Jeffery Curtis, and Follow MeJeffery Curtis PoorHusband. Father. Pastor. Church Planter. Writer. Trying to be more like Jesus each day. BA in Biblical Studies - Ozark Christian College (2012) MA in Theology - Regent University (2019) Email Me: Email. "The Powerful Meaning of James 1:2-4 (Count It All Joy)." Rethink, October 19, 2023. https://www.rethinknow.org/meaning-of-james-1-2-4-count-it-all-joy/.

Staff, BibleStudyTools. "James 4:11-12 - Brothers and Sisters, Do Not Slander One Another. ..." Bible Study Tools. Accessed May 27, 2024. https://www.biblestudytools.com/james/passage/?q=james%2B4%3A11-12.

"What Does James 1:11 Mean?" Verse of the day. Accessed April 29, 2024. https://dailyverse.knowing-jesus.com/james-1-11.

Wilkin, Bob. "Faith without Works Is Dead - James 2:14-17." Grace Evangelical Society, June 30, 2017. https://faithalone.org/blog/faith-without-works-is-dead/.